out of pr

A LITTLE THING CALLED PRIDE

A Little Thing called Pride

Alec Stock

An Autobiography

Pelham Books

First published in Great Britain by
Pelham Books Ltd
44 Bedford Square
London WC1B 3DU
1982

British Library Cataloguing in Publication Data
Stock, Alec
A little thing called pride.
1. Stock, Alec 2. Soccer managers–Great Britain–Autobiography
I. Title
796.334'092'4 GV942.7.S/

ISBN 0 7207 1395 1

Typeset by Saildean Ltd, Surrey.
Printed and bound by Billing & Sons Ltd,
Guildford, London and Worcester

Contents

Foreword by Rodney Marsh

Alec Stock glared at me from the foot of the trainer's table in the Queen's Park Rangers medical room. He looked toward Ron Woolnough, the QPR physio. 'How is he?' he asked in his patented preoccupied manner. 'It looks like he may have broken a bone in his foot Alec,' Ron offered apologetically. 'He can't have,' countered Alec gruffly. 'He's my No.10.'

We were about to play Cardiff City in a crucial Second Division promotion battle at Ninian Park, and 'the Boss', as every player without exception affectionately called him, was very much aware of its importance. 'Fitness test!' His tone had changed to a demanding roar.

Now, as anyone associated with professional soccer will testify, a fitness test usually consists of running, jumping, twisting, turning, sprinting, and ball work. Alec told Ron and me to wait on the field for him and he would be out right away. We waited patiently in the goalmouth. Suddenly, out came the boss with a ball which he threw towards us from the touchline. It rolled slowly across the QPR mud and came to an abrupt halt about twenty yards from the goal at the top of the penalty area arch. He followed it to where Ron and I were standing.

'OK Rod, smash the ball at the goal!' No warm up. No stretching. I bent down to place the ball. It was flat, a three-year-old kid could have kicked it over the stands. I was still snickering to myself as I ran towards it. As the ball exploded into the roof of the net I screamed in agony. Alec glanced across towards the physio. 'See Ron. He's fit.'

I suppose some players, past and present, might be disturbed at being treated that way. But I guess Alec knew that I would take it as the supreme compliment. I had total respect and admiration for 'the boss' and always will have. Two words come to mind in any account of Alec Stock's career ... Pride and Dignity.

Rodney Marsh
November 1981

Introduction by Brian Woolnough

There will always be a corner in football history for Alec Stock. It will not be reserved for him alongside other managers of his era, winners like Busby, Nicholson, Shankly, Ramsey, Clough or Paisley. Stock will have a place all of his own marked 'Miracle Man', the manager with the midas touch.

A modest and highly sensitive person, Stock is embarrassed by his label, although he admits he has had great satisfaction and a lot of fun out of taking something small and moulding it into a much bigger and better object. Ever since he led Southern League Yeovil to the fifth round of the FA Cup in January 1949, football has expected that little bit extra from 'good old Alec' and he has responded with great feats for Orient, Queen's Park Rangers, Luton and Fulham. Players like Rodney Marsh and Malcolm Macdonald would never have played for England had it not been for Stock's unique style of management.

Anyone who has met Stock and talked football with him will have already been captivated by his style. 'Hello old son, lovely, lovely, come in, have a gin and tonic ... it's not a bad old life is it? ... Hmmm.'

It is impossible to dislike the man. He prides himself on always being fair with players and he always gives the company and the situation he is in an air of respectability. 'How do you argue with Alec Stock?' Malcolm Macdonald once said: 'He listens, he talks sense, and in the end you do what he says.'

Macdonald recalls his first team talk with Stock as a Luton player with a great deal of pleasure. 'There was no pressure, no confusion. Alec just walked in about half an hour before the kick-off and said: "OK fellas. It's a lovely day and, quite frankly, football is a simple game. The crowd want to have a bit of fun and there is no reason why we shouldn't give it to them, hmmm. When you are walking out think about yourselves and what the crowd are expecting. It's all about a little thing called pride, isn't it? Hmmm, hmmm." And with that he was gone, leaving coach Jimmy Andrews to tidy up the tactics.'

If there is one word that Stock likes to be associated with it is 'respect'. He has always demanded it and given it. People have continually turned to him for an opinion and he has become one of the wise old men of football. He admits: 'I will cry the day they stop asking me my opinion.' He eats, sleeps, and drinks football and only loses his self-control when others knock the game he loves so much. That is the reason why I was delighted to give him all the help I could in writing this book. Apart from its being a story of interesting achievement, it is a book of strong and controversial opinion. He really cares about the future of English football.

While Stock was manager of Luton one of his directors was comedian Eric Morecambe. When I asked him to describe Stock he said:

> He is a gentleman, and that is the nicest thing you can say about him, or anyone come to that. I look upon him as a friend as well as being one of our former managers. They were happy days at Luton when Alec was in charge and he built us a damn good side. With a bit of luck he might still have been manager of Luton and have taken us into the First Division. He often looked dour but had a very dry sense of humour. I can still see him now standing at the front of the coach and leading the singing, win or lose. Alec loved a singsong. I'm sure it helped him unwind after the matches.

There is a little story that I remember so well that sums up Alec Stock for me. We had just lost a vital home game in the Second Division that probably meant we were not going to go up. I used to stay behind for a couple of hours after the game for a drink and a chat with a few of the blokes who knew something about football. It was a bit of an education for me.

As Alec was leaving on this particular occasion, I opened the boardroom door for him. He obviously thought no one was behind him because he gave the chair on top of the stairs an almighty kick that sent it hurtling across the landing. It was his private moment of pressure release, and I thought, 'my goodness, that's the torture he has been going through since the end of the game.' Yet he never once showed it in public. He always handled himself well when it mattered.

He is at Bournemouth now, isn't he. Good luck to him. I bet I know what he is going through – he is probably missing the pressure. I'm sure he still wants to be involved. At least he has got some sunshine though, he can't be missing the Luton fog!

It is true that Stock does miss the pressure. He has always loved things happening around him, especially in London. And he has carried on despite his deafness and asthma, two handicaps that might have forced many of us to give up years ago. There is absolutely no chance of getting one of Stock's players to knock 'the boss'. Vic Groves, a player Stock discovered for Leyton Orient and eventually sold to Arsenal, once said to me, 'If you are writing about Alec Stock don't you dare say anything nasty.'

Mark Lazarus, whom Stock signed three times during his career, recalls one important promotion match. 'We were winning easily at half-time and Alec strode into the dressing-room as proud as Punch. He has always worn a pork pie cap and I'd had my eye on this particular one for weeks. It was obvious we were going to win so I began to lark about and took off his hat and said I was going out for the second half wearing it. Alec turned on us all and said “Now look, we haven’t won this yet ... but if we do I will take you all down to Dunns in the morning and buy you each one of these”, holding up his cap. And sure enough the very next day we were all in Dunns trying on hats and caps. That kind of thing only endears a manager to his players.’

My own favourite story about Alec Stock dates back to the Wednesday before Fulham’s unexpected FA Cup Final appearance at Wembley in 1975. Alec strode out onto Craven Cottage, immaculately dressed as always, to take a look at the training. The players were having a five-a-side practice match and goalkeeper Peter Mellor, who had decided to try his hand at centre forward, scored just as Stock appeared. ‘Beat that Alec’ Mellor said jokingly. I can still see the players’ faces as Alec put a ball down on the corner flag and sent it curling from his highly polished shoe right into the top corner of the net. ‘OK fellas, carry on’ he said. ‘Never lose it, do you. Hmmm.’ And that is Stock. A mixture of mischief and enthusiasm – respect and style.

At the start of the 1981-82 season he handed over the running of the Bournemouth team to former Chelsea player David Well, and the club promptly made Alec a director. At the age of sixty-five it kept him involved with the sport he loves. He was certainly not ready to bow out. It will be a sad day for football if Stock’s experience and opinions are not used in some capacity. As he says himself: ‘Never really want to stop, do I? Quite frankly, you have got to keep going, haven’t you. It’s not been a bad old life though, has it? Hmmm. Hmmm.’

1 You call that Loyalty?

There was only one thing on my mind that grey Sunday morning in November 1968 as I drove towards Queen's Park Rangers ground in West London. I wanted to start work again. For the first time in two long months I felt completely fit, clear again from the asthma attack that had struck me down just as I was about to enjoy the proudest moment of my career; being in charge of a team in the First Division.

What I could see from the outside was that the team I had taken through the Third Division into the First, a side so good it made me excited every time I thought about it, needed me back. They had started so disastrously in the First Division, losing six games and drawing five. I couldn't understand what had gone wrong, why Marsh, Keen, Sibley, Allen, Sanderson and the rest, who had grown stronger and better by the month, were struggling. Teams don't suddenly lose everything overnight.

As I drew up outside the main entrance behind chairman Jim Gregory's Rolls-Royce my mind went back to March of the previous year, to a marvellous day in Queen's Park Rangers history when they became the first Third Division club to win the League Cup, coming from 0-2 down at half-time against First Division West Bromwich Albion with three goals after the interval.

It was a fantastic feeling of achievement for the players and for me. The party mood lapped over to the following Tuesday when we were at home to Bournemouth. Strangely

I was nervous, there was no need for me to be edgy but I wanted promotion just as much as the League Cup and I remember hoping for two points as my wife Marjorie and I drove to Loftus Road. There was no need for me to have worried. We were brilliant, winning 4-0; although in the end that night was to turn my career upside down and eventually result in my being sacked by a club who had said I would stay with them for the rest of my life.

As expected after our Wembley triumph, the ground was bursting at the seams hours before the kick-off and I couldn't park my car in the usual place, leaving it instead 400 yards away from the main entrance.

As I have already said, we were superb, with Marshy at his brilliant arrogant best. He swept in two goals from outside the area and I was enjoying the game so much I recall shouting at the referee just before the end: 'Let it run another twenty minutes, let the crowd have some more entertainment.' It was that kind of night, a great game, a few gin and tonics and even this outrageous comment from a chairman. 'That Marsh is a lucky player.' 'Lucky', I said, 'That was his thirty-ninth goal of the season, more than your own team has scored.'

It was raining when Marjorie and I left the ground so I ran on ahead to get my car. After a few steps I was struggling. I couldn't catch my breath, there was a pain in my chest. 'What have I done?', I said to myself. 'I can't breathe properly.' The pain hadn't improved when we got home and I didn't sleep a wink that night. It was my first bad attack of asthma, a complaint that stayed with me from that moment on.

It was a real struggle to get through the remainder of our promotion season, even harder in 1967-68 when we went up to the First Division thanks to an own goal on the very last Saturday. There were many days when I had to hide my condition from the players and I remember coming home from floodlit matches and just sitting up all night. They were pretty difficult times, but we survived as a family and a club and we went up. I had got QPR right the way through from the Third to the First Division.

During the summer I tried to get to the bottom of my problem, I so desperately wanted to pin up that first team on the opening day of the season. I did the rounds of specialists and finished up in the Brompton Hospital where a doctor delivered an analysis I didn't want to hear. 'You have overworked, old son, take three months off.' 'Three months', I said, 'I can't afford to be out of work that long'. I immediately went home and suffered my worst asthma attack. So I was carted back to hospital and stayed there when the season – that season I had dreamt about from the day I entered management with Southern League Yeovil in 1946 – kicked off.

For someone who is a bit of a worryguts and a workaholic it was a nightmare, especially on Saturday afternoons. I felt cut off and lonely. And at the back of my mind there was Jim Gregory. My mind kept going back to the club's chairman, a very ambitious man. He had been good for the club from the start, injecting enough money to keep my side together, persuading me to stay eighteen months before the League Cup triumph when I thought about resigning, and then financing a number of deals.

But the more success we had the more I felt that Jim fancied himself as the manager. And there was one thing in the way, me. Jim knew that I always had to be the boss of the team. My fears only got worse when no one came to see me in hospital or at home as I was convalescing, and then, at the Secretary and Managers Dinner in London, I discovered that Jim had offered the manager's job to Bill Dodgin, my number two.

I should have quit there and then and put myself on the market. But I didn't and clung to my team. I knew that given the chance the players and I could pick up from the club's disastrous start. I began to drift back on Saturdays to watch from the grandstand, but I felt like a stranger. It was an anticlimax, I had no control over what was going on.

Yet on that Sunday morning I was full of optimism again. I had been to see a junior game and knew that Jim Gregory would be at the ground. 'I want to see you a minute Alec,' he said. I thought he was going to welcome me back with open arms. I thought and hoped he was going to say, 'Come on Alec, glad to have you back, let's get this show on the road again.' But he didn't and twenty seconds later I was out, sacked with this damning testimony. 'You are ill, you're incurable, I want you to go.'

There is not much you can do or say in situations like that, you just want to get out. A thousand things rush through your mind in that split second. I remember thinking 'Twenty-one years I have waited to get in the First Division, and it's taken just twenty seconds to kick me out. And why say I'm ill, why not give me the chop with a bit of dignity, why must there always be a rotten reason for going?'

The directors sacking a manager never say: 'We have done a rotten filthy trick'. They just push out the man they chose, in such a callous way that he feels as if he has had his fingers in the petty cash. To make my exit even sadder, Jim had to bargain over the £5,000 the club owed me. 'I'll give you four' he said. It makes you cry, doesn't it. Everything has got to be a deal, and it's a deal when only one man wins.

Why! Was I so unreasonable? I had just given the best years of my life to that club. They eventually gave me £4,500 and I turned my back on a team that had been my life. The effect of that twenty-second interview on my family was disastrous. My daughters Elizabeth and Sarah were shocked and bitter for weeks and Marjorie probably summed up how I felt with this statement: 'Alec' she said, when I returned to our Epsom, Surrey home, 'We only found rubbish at the top of our mountain'.

I have never asked Jim Gregory the real reasons why he sacked me, I suppose my pride took over. There is no doubt that Queen's Park Rangers owe a lot to Gregory but at that moment I thought they owed a bit to me. Jim will no doubt say he did it for the good of the club and, in the end, who can argue? He is the chairman, the boss, one of the most powerful men in soccer. Powerful because he is the chairman of a football club.

And that is the theme of this book, my life story. It is also the theme of football. It is about people, the style and quality of chairmen and directors – the men who make decisions. It is about the calibre of person who eventually dictates the standard of quality and the future of this game. It is also about members of the Management Committee and the Football Association Council. Because football as you see it at this moment is a reflection of the people at the top and it's a very sad scene.

When I was sacked by Queen's Park Rangers I realized for the first time the power of the football club chairman. You begin to wonder if these people obtain power too quickly, too easily. Should they be able to sack when they feel like it, ruining a man's career in twenty seconds? Jim Gregory has always been his own man, choosing the manager, directors and – players? – he wanted around him and moving them over if he thought they stood in the way of progress. He has certainly always known what he wanted.

I returned to Queen's Park Rangers in June 1981 for the opening of their £350,000 artificial turf pitch. It was the first of its kind in football and when I stood out in the middle on the 'Magic Carpet', and looked around me and saw the enclosed ground and executive boxes, I thought about Jim Gregory again. I thought that this is what Jim probably always hoped for. His club. His stadium. Yes, I handed it to my former chairman that day. He may be ruthless but he has used it to make progress. There are undoubtedly a lot of people who are envious of what he has done at Queen's Park Rangers.

That Sunday afternoon after being sacked I sat at home wondering what the future held. How often can a manager build a club up from nothing again? Luton gave me the answer and a month later I was building from the bottom once more, driving for six days a week from Epsom to Kenilworth Road and back.

I threw myself into the Luton job and that was a direct swipe at QPR. I wanted to prove to them and to the rest of football that I was fit. Every time I got on the M1 motorway I smiled to myself 'Go on old son, keep going.' The miracle began to work again and I believe that the Luton side I built could have done even better than Rangers. Malcolm Macdonald, Don Givens, Mike Keen, Graham French – it was not a bad old team and we were purring our way through the Second Division. I was on course to get from the Third to the First without stopping again when bad luck struck me down once more.

Tony Hunt, the club's very good chairman, had a lot of money tied up in the Vehicle and General Insurance Company and when they went bust my world crashed again. I was asked to find a quarter of a million pounds overnight and Macdonald was sold to Newcastle. I immediately ran into more boardroom disloyalty and walked out, another four years' hard work gone up in smoke and for the second time I had lost a damn good side.

People have called me the man who turned unknown players into stars and helped small clubs discover the big time and I am proud of that record. But it is hard when little empires and years of slog are whisked away overnight. A football manager's job is like no other in any line of business. Where else would you find so much disloyalty? Where else would a man's career be severed after working so hard for one company? How many men in business walk away with nothing after making so much for other people?

Fulham came next and, amazingly, we started to build again. It climaxed with the 1975 FA Cup Final against West Ham. Deep down I knew that would be my last little miracle. Even Marjorie said 'That's it Alec. Don't care any more'. What she meant was that I had really proved myself and at the age of fifty-eight should sit back. But I *did* care, especially when boardroom politics began to slice Fulham apart. Again I saw disloyalty, I saw people with little knowledge and feeling for the game, who wanted control of a football club for their own ego, their own business interest.

Loyalty has been a key word throughout my career. I'm probably a bit too old-fashioned, too naïve. I think everyone is nice in football. And, believe me, it is a mistake to think that.

I have had many regrets throughout my career but like to think I have contributed my little corner to football. It worries me that there are too many men around today who are happy to take but not to give. They include some chairmen, a lot of directors, and men sitting on influential committees. It is they who must make decisions to rescue this game in the next ten years.

2 Chairmen and Directors

Bertie Mee, the former Arsenal manager who led his club to the League and Cup double in 1971, produced a staggering piece of information at the end of the 1980-81 season. He worked out that the average life of a manager at a Football Club was down to two and a half years. That, I'm afraid, is a terrible reflection on the changing image of the game. It is an image that no one, quite frankly, should be proud of and the accusing finger must be pointed at the new breed of club chairmen and directors.

They are a ruthless bunch who put business and balance sheets before the game and stick their own ego out in front of loyalty and dedication to the sport. These are men who sack managers when they feel like it and then play a game of lucky dip before coming up with a new face. I have often been asked, 'Why didn't you apply for our job?' The answer is simple, 'Surely you must have known who you wanted?'

They are not all the same, thank God, and the marvellous thing about 1981 is that most of the good guys won. The nice guys, the clubs and managers with a bit of style and dignity. Liverpool, Ipswich, West Ham, Spurs, clubs who don't chop and change, directors who don't bow to public pressure; they forced their way out in front. And believe me, we have got to hope they stay there.

If they are swamped, and the hard-headed businessmen who see themselves as club owners start overtaking, we have got no chance. The rest of football will say: 'They have done it overnight, we want to be like them.' And there will be a sharp deterioration in the standards of our game. In the end there will be no style left.

I have always thought that it is too easy to become a chairman or director. That fear has grown recently. I worry that the old patron of sport as we once knew him is now losing his role in football to the moneymaker, the man who sits in his office with lawyers and solicitors doing all the deals until one day he decides he wants to be noticed. He is doing well but wants the public to realize just what a success of his life he is making.

If his outlet is football he doesn't have much trouble in buying some shares in a big club and before long he is the major shareholder and therefore a club owner. He has got his power, his game, his business empire, call it what you like. He is a person more concerned about assets than building a club, he is a man with too much power.

Some directors are a very disloyal bunch of men. They listen to gossip and whispers, they become unsettled by a couple of bad results; today they haven't learned to cope with winning and losing which, after all, is what this great game is all about. They can destroy a manager's career overnight and, quite frankly, they should never have that kind of power. I believe it was Brian Clough who once said he was tired of building up an empire for other people. There is nothing left for a manager when he goes, no cut of the business he has made, no reward, and certainly no thanks.

I have encountered disloyalty twice in my career. At Rangers and then again at Luton where things went wrong overnight after the Vehicle and General collapse. Our chairman, Tony Hunt, was a major influence on the rise of Luton Town, he was a personality, a man with a bit of style who allowed us to get on with the running of the club.

Tony Hunt was ill when things started to go wrong and a great boardroom row developed behind his back. I was asked to raise £250,000 overnight, Macdonald and then others were sold and Tony, who had been the blue-eyed boy only a couple of weeks earlier, was suddenly the villain. And through it all only one director stood firm alongside me, Eric Morecambe. He knew where his loyalties lay, he knew that Hunt had done so much for Luton.

With the other directors I saw disloyalty again, I discovered to my horror that they had no dignity. Those men should have rallied round Tony Hunt, instead they let their little ambitions show. You could hear their minds ticking over 'I could be chairman here. I haven't got any qualifications but wouldn't the wife be proud of me.' They started to talk about the team, they wanted to know if we were going to win something. 'Gentlemen' I said, 'Haven't we just sold our best players?' Then they turned on Jimmy Andrews, our coach who had done so much for the Luton players.

At Fulham I witnessed what was perhaps the biggest boardroom tug-of-war of all. My head spins now with all that went on in a very short time behind the scenes at Craven Cottage; it was a chapter of events that turned a lovely club into just another name on the pools coupon. People used to go to Fulham because the club was different, it was a club with something about it. Yes, Fulham had style. But not any longer, and do the new directors really care?

Ernie Clay, a tough millionaire businessman who years earlier had helped George Eastham give football the maximum wage, brought the first winds of change to Fulham. And dear old Fulham was never the same after Mr Clay's arrival. On his first day he announced to the players at training 'We shall all be rich one day when we have a BUPA Hospital and Hotel on the ground.' The only thing I could think of was that he had plans to sell up – the ground was allegedly valued at £8 million in 1976 – and move us to another part of London.

Things like that only succeed in putting doubt into other people's minds, it is very difficult to manage a club when you are looking over your shoulder waiting for the next bombshell. The chairman must be responsible for everything that happens in his club and the manager, therefore, should have complete confidence in his employer. But it doesn't always work out like that.

The next bombshell was Malcolm Macdonald's contract. Clay and the late Sir Eric Miller suddenly produced Macdonald's contract at a board meeting. He was a Newcastle player but they said they were going to prove in the High Court that the contract was null and void and that, in two months, Fulham would be signing England's centre forward on a free transfer. My reply to them would be unprintable, but I did add 'You must be joking' and 'I have almost had enough of you lot'. For some reason Macdonald had allowed himself to become the fall guy for a high-powered battle; they wanted to prove that Newcastle couldn't retain Malcolm as a player once his contract had expired.

Well, that stank to me, it was far from right in my book. In all my wildest dreams I just don't imagine people to be like that. Maybe I'm old fashioned but when things go cock-eyed I walk away. And, eventually, that is what I did.

After that board meeting I contacted Harry Haslam, an old friend of Macdonald's. I asked Harry what the hell was going on and, thankfully, after he spoke to Malcolm, our friend signed for Arsenal. I was delighted because it wouldn't have done him any good to get involved with what Clay and Miller had in mind.

There was one clause in Macdonald's contract however that did make me sit up and wonder just how many rules are being broken. Newcastle were paying him a bonus if he scored thirty or more goals each season. It was a unique agreement as far as I was concerned and what a beautiful thing for a manager to have. Wouldn't we all like to have signed a centre forward and given him that kind of incentive. It was only at the start of the 1981-82 season that the Football League allowed clubs to pay their strikers for goals.

Before I couldn't understand why no one else was allowed to use a similar agreement and the late Alan Hardaker, the former Football League Secretary, would always say Football League regulations didn't allow it. Again I have to ask the question, why? It makes you wonder.

Board meetings at Fulham were never the same after that. All conversation concentrated on how to teach Hardaker and Football Association Secretary Ted Croker how to run the game rather than repairing the image and getting Fulham into the First Division. Another decision the board made that only widened the gap between me and them had been over Alan Mullery, our skipper, and a player I signed for £62,500 from Spurs eventually to take over the playing side from me.

He had captained us at Wembley, was voted the Football Writers' Player of the Year, appeared on *This is Your Life,* received the MBE and was the BBC's *'Goal of the Year'* competition winner. But suddenly Sir Eric Miller said he didn't like Mullery and didn't want him as coach. In one swoop my planning for Fulham's future had been knocked sideways by someone with the power to make big decisions.

A football match was never won in the boardroom and I have never met anyone upstairs with as much knowledge about my side as I have. No one in the boardroom knows enough about players to pick teams and staff so I was bitterly disappointed that Fulham didn't keep Mullery.

Being a director is also not the expensive game people think. At all my clubs I have never known a director lose money. If they put some cash in they can take it out when the going gets tough, or demand that a player be sold. No manager likes to sell, and when he does it is usually done to balance out some internal problem.

One of the best chairmen I worked for was Bert Smith at Yeovil who had a really deep feeling for the game. It is the kind of gut feeling that Bert had which is so essential for anyone who cares.

My first chairman at QPR, Bert Hessinger, was also a marvellous man. You had to be at his board meetings to appreciate how tough and complicated life with directors has become today. Bert's meetings would start at 7.30 and by eight o'clock he would be telling me about the day he took five catches behind the wicket for his local club cricket side. Those Rangers directors couldn't even have told you who

Chelsea, their neighbours, were playing the next day. All they wanted was for their club to improve and have a good image in the game.

Then, of course, there was dear Harry Zussman at Orient, a beautiful front man for his club who treated football with a great deal of fun. Football lost a great character when Harry sadly and suddenly died in July 1981. He let his manager run the show completely and was as good a loser as I have met. When I first joined Leyton Orient in May 1949 Harry was chairman because he had the most money invested in the club, something in the region of £1,500. He didn't have a deep knowledge of the game but was a very good man to work for. I loved working for Orient and Zussman was the main reason I went back three times.

It was also damned hard work, twenty times harder than Yeovil. We never had any money and our sole asset at the start was a secondhand lawn mower. The club even advertised for directors at £750 each. The summers were one long headache as we scrambled around finding enough money to get through the close season period.

Inevitably clubs like Orient have to sell and when Arsenal made an approach for Vic Groves and Stan Charlton it was too good an opportunity to miss. The trouble was we were top of the Third Division and the sale at such an important time for the club gave everyone, from Harry Zussman down, the shakes. Our next match after that deal was away to Aldershot and Harry knew how vital it was for us not to lose, the fans would have gone mad, probably calling for our heads.

As we were having a cup of tea on Waterloo Station waiting for the train to Aldershot, Harry said to me 'Alec, I would give a few bob to get something today'. It just so happened that a few yards away in the buffet and travelling on the same train, was Ted Platt, the Aldershot goalkeeper who used to live next door to our assistant secretary John Smith (now chief executive with Luton Town) and who also trained with us. 'Well there's your chance' I said to Harry. 'That's Ted Platt over there.'

The match against Aldershot was very keen. Jimmy Sirrell was playing for them and it was a sharp old game to say the least. We threw everything at Platt all afternoon without success and with ten minutes to go Aldershot led 1-0. Then Platt, having played a blinder, kicked a goalkick straight at our centre forward Mike Burgess on the edge of the area and we got the point we desperately needed.

All hell broke out from that moment, the Aldershot players started to argue. Platt was suddenly the culprit and there was a lot of pushing and shoving as the players came off the pitch. One player needed stitches as Platt lashed out and in their dressing-room the club doctor finished up under the billiard table. The outcome was that on the following Monday, Platt was sold to Worcester City and the next time I saw Harry he said: 'Alec, you didn't, did you?' But that point was good enough for Harry, he was happy when things were going smoothly.

A few days later we played Crystal Palace at home and within five minutes we were 4-0 up. Their goalkeeper finished up injured at centre forward and we went on to win 8-0. So all worked out well. We were forgiven for selling Groves and Charlton.

If that gamble had failed I'm sure Harry Zussman and his board would still have backed me. Today in a similar position and at a different club, I would not be so confident. Too many directors today want instant success, they want a manager with a magic wand, they want trophies tomorrow. It means you are living in a pressure-cooker all the time and it's getting to the stage when two weeks bad work can count as a failure for a manager.

He knows that he has got to get it right quickly and keep the ship on course. That can only result in one thing, frightened management; frightened to lose. Those kind of chairmen and directors are setting the standard of the game and, at the moment, it is not a standard to be proud of.

How marvellous that a club like Ipswich are being rewarded for their loyalty to Bobby Robson. They have stuck by him, never put him under pressure, always supported him and can now sit back and say: 'We were right'. I wonder how many sacked managers could have done a Robson at their own clubs, given more time and support.

I often wonder if directors are frightened of managers, frightened of their knowledge, of their personality. Why is it that we don't get more former managers becoming directors; their knowledge would surely be valuable? Their qualifications are far greater than most directors; come to that what *is* the qualification of a director? It is just a role in sport that gives them a marvellous, beautiful life. They are glorified spectators with too much power. Well, that power is being challenged at last, their selfishness is being challenged. They must move over or get out of the game.

Football desperately needs an injection of dignity and style, men who care about the game and not themselves. But if the wrong men stay in power I cry for the future of football.

3 Its Not a Bad Old Life

It was Christmas Day in Yeovil. The year escapes me but this particular occasion doesn't. All the Yeovil players, chairman Bert Smith, some directors and I were enjoying a good old-fashioned knees-up in a pub called the Nags Head.

Players were singing round the piano, the champagne was flowing and we were full up with turkey and the usual trimmings. At five o'clock with the party at its peak I suddenly realized that we had a Southern League match in the morning and this, really, wasn't the ideal preparation. I needn't have worried, we were superb on Boxing Day, winning 9-0.

I'm not pushing that forward as the ideal or indeed my idea of a match build-up but it is a good little cameo of how I have treated players throughout my career. What would have been the point in refusing those Yeovil players a drink or celebration. It was Christmas Day, they would have resented being told 'No' and perhaps not responded the next day. Certainly I would have gone down in their estimation. I must admit when I looked at my watch and discovered it was so late I thought 'Oh hell, this doesn't often happen. It's not a bad old life.'

All through my career I have been proud of my relationship with players. I have always treated them as equals, like men, I have never asked a player to do what I would have refused to do as a player. And I like to think I have been rewarded with not one angry transfer demand, not one row or bitter reaction towards me in the press.

Men respond to being treated fairly, that's something I learned in the Army as a member of the Northampton Yeomanry. 'Thou shalt not bleat' was our motto. 'Face up, Own up' – it's not a bad policy. I loved every minute of the Army, it taught me what to say, when to say it and how to say it.

My squadron leader once asked me to defend a man who had been court-martialled for Absence Without Leave. 'But Sir' I said. 'I have never done anything like this before.' That didn't seem to matter and he just said, 'You come from Bath don't you, well he is from Bristol, you probably speak the same language.' The soldier got six months in the glasshouse and thanked me profusely!

The war also took its toll physically. I stopped a bazooka in the back and ended up in a nursing home for three months. I soon got talking to the man in the next bed and we dreamed away the hours talking about football and other sports. He turned out to be the late J. L. Manning, the former Fleet Street sports writer.

I also broke my wrist (an injury which forced me to give up cricket, damn it) and as I didn't use ear plugs as a gunning officer I am partially deaf. If you couple my deafness with my asthma you can appreciate there have been long days of discomfort for me.

My asthma, however, had nothing to do with the war. It was caused and then aggravated, the experts say, by years of shouting and screaming at players during training. I have not found asthma difficult to live with and it has been my deafness that has been far more inconvenient. I have never heard a referee's whistle from my seat alongside the pitch. That, you may argue, is not such a bad thing. But I don't hear the birds sing either!

I also lose high-frequency voices and that has meant a problem when talking to women. I have been known to walk away suddenly from a group of women and this obviously appears rude. But it has just been because the conversation was impossible to follow. I have been advised many times to use a deaf aid but have never brought myself to wear one. You can imagine the stick I would have taken walking onto the training ground wearing a deaf aid and wheezing. The players would probably have thought I was tied together with string.

From my first day to the day I ended my service, as a captain, the Army was good for Alec William Stock. It was the best thing to happen to me as a grounding for management, and the tactics were similar. We were always told, attack like hell when you can.

It also taught me discipline, another vital part of running a football club, and it made every soldier have a pride in their appearance. I just don't understand why footballers today look so scruffy in public. Certain clubs allow their players to wander around as if they were all going to a pop concert. It appals me and certainly no player of mine has been scruffily turned out.

There was one player who made me feel proud and that was Bobby Moore, the former England World Cup captain whom I signed for Fulham from West Ham. Moore was a big man in every sense of the word and he was always immaculately dressed. There is no doubt about it, Moore had style. Fulham used to train at Tolworth in Surrey and that meant an hour and a half drive for him, but you could bet your mortgage that Bob would be there on time.

I can see him now after matches, sitting still in the dressing-room as everyone else flew around. Then after about ten minutes he would get out a big piece of cotton wool and start to clean his boots. And he wouldn't finish until they were spotless, as clean as when he put them on just before the kick-off. It was sheer pride, good habits, good upbringing, from the maestro. Call it what you like, Moore had it. Other players not in Moore's class would just throw down their boots hoping for someone else to clean them.

After going to the rugby-playing Dartford Grammar School I was seventeen before I took part in my first serious game of soccer. I was a trainee bank clerk and football management was certainly not on my mind during those first matches for Wilmington Village and Redhill.

My first break and link with professional football came during a spell of three games for Spurs as an amateur. Jimmy Seed, the famous Charlton manager, approached me after one match and offered me a contract. I decided to sign but with the condition that my father, John Stock, a miner most of his life, was taken on as assistant groundsman. Reed agreed and I had broken into football, playing alongside two men who were to become good old friends, the late Bert Tann and Fred Ford.

I stayed at Charlton for two years before moving across London to Queen's Park Rangers and they were happy times at the Valley. The memories came flooding back in June of 1981 with the sad death of Bert Turner.

Bert was an immaculate, big man, over six foot tall and fifteen stone of muscle. His only problem was that every summer he would put on weight and turn up for the first day of training a stone too heavy. Well, at Charlton in those days they had a huge boiler at the back of the dressing-room and that's where Bert always ended up. He was stripped off, had two old red tyre inner tubes fastened to his middle, and was ordered to skip for hours in a track suit, two jumpers and a towel tucked into his neck! 'That'll teach you Bert', Seed would say.

At the end of my military service, Marjorie and I lived in Somerset, not a great distance from my home at Peasedown, a village near Bath. I was completely torn about what to do with my life. Should I stay in football or go back to banking?

I used to keep fit by digging the garden. At the same time I would turn over in my mind what to do for the best. My wife came up with the answer in the form of an advertisement in the local paper. 'Yeovil want a player-manager' she said. 'You could get that.' I wasn't sure but then Clifford Webb, the sports columnist, reported that football was going to take off again and so I decided to apply. Yeovil had sixty applicants and I was lucky enough to get the job. It was 1946 and the door had been opened to me. My life in management had begun.

I say it was a lucky day but now I wouldn't take a player-manager's job if the salary was £20,000 a year and not the £7 a week I was paid when I started. It's damn hard work and my advice to anyone contemplating starting a career as a player-manager today is don't.

I survived on hope and work. I hoped it would be a nice day and so a few more people would come through the turnstile, I hoped all the players would turn up, I hoped they would play well and that I would be OK.

I only saw my players on match days and spent the week worrying if they were keeping fit. They had to be paid, of course, and after each home game I would rush out of the dressing-room to help the chairman envelope up the wages and then count the gate money. Match day was a long hard slog that began with mowing the grass and marking the lines out on the pitch. There was just enough time at the end for a couple of gin and tonics with the chairman before trudging home.

My three years at Yeovil, of course, were smashing experience and happy times. And despite the hard slog I like to think we turned Yeovil from a Southern League side into a household name with our run to the FA Cup fifth round.

During that Cup journey I began to get our sloping pitch as much publicity as possible and by the time Bury arrived for the third round the entire country thought we played on the side of a house. On match day morning I looked out of my tiny office and there were the Bury players, running up the slope, measuring crosses, sprinting down it. They were worried stiff and from that moment I knew we didn't have any problems.

When mighty Sunderland arrived the entire county was locked in one big carnival. Everyone wanted to see the slope, everyone wanted to see Sunderland lose. Stan Hall, our goalkeeper, injured his knee on a bottle-top a day before the kick-off while jumping around for photographers and I was forced to throw in a kid called Dicky Dyke. Young Dick did so well that I signed him for £3 10s a week on the Monday after we had knocked out Sunderland.

Sunderland didn't really want to run and sweat during the game, they didn't have the appetite, and after I scored in the thirtieth minute I had a fancy we were heading for one of the great upsets of all time. But they managed to equalize and the match went into extra time. Eric Bryant put us into the lead again and you could feel the tension as the crowd prayed for the final whistle. As one of my defenders kicked the ball out of the ground Len Shackleton turned to me and said, 'Don't spoil a good game'. 'A game,' I replied, 'This is life and death to us.'

Then, in the last seconds, Sunderland were awarded a free kick on the edge of the area and I called the entire Yeovil team back to make a defensive wall. As Barney Ramsden, who was about 6ft 4in and had a shot like a rocket, ran up to take it I turned to my team and said: 'Gentlemen, anyone who ducks will be sacked.' No one did and I needn't have worried, Ramsden's shot ended up in the allotments behind the goal. We went on to lose 0-8 to Manchester United in the fifth round but it didn't matter, Yeovil had arrived, we were on the map.

I have only fond memories of Yeovil. The people were nice, they were characters, sincere folk who lived for each other. There were plenty of strong characters around too, like Don Filer, my brother-in-law. His character came out during one match for Shoscombe in the Bath and District League Division Four.

Don was a farmer and every match day he would change at home and walk through the cobbled streets in his gear, his big long wooden studs knocking on the pavement. He got some strange looks, especially if it was raining and he put his long mac on over his gear. But Don didn't mind, he loved his football. On this particular Saturday Shoscombe were playing Bath Rovers in a local derby and after a ding dong first half, Don was unfortunate enough to get sent off. Well, at 4.15 on a Saturday afternoon there is only one thing a farmer thinks of if he is not involved with sport, and that's milking time.

So Don marched from the pitch straight into an adjoining

field and what happened next can only be described as unique. My brother-in-law became the only man in football history to get suspended for life for chasing the referee off the field of play with a tractor!

It ended the game, of course, although the Bath skipper was quite good about it. In a letter to Shoscombe he wrote: 'The sending off incident didn't worry us too much but we found it a bit disconcerting in the second half when, every time we attacked, a man standing next to the goal fired a sawn-off shot gun over the heads of our forwards.' No one discovered however if that was Don as well.

There are some people it seems who can't forget my relationship with Yeovil. I did a little interview for the BBC about Yeovil for their Centenary programme before the 1981 Cup Final between Spurs and Manchester City. They said they would pop a cheque for £25 in the post and I thought nothing more of it. A few weeks later the cheque turned up at Yeovil Football Club. I rang the BBC and said: 'You're thirty-five years out of date, old son.'

I joined Orient, known then as Leyton Orient, in August 1949 and my opening speech to the players is something I have repeated to all the men I have worked with. I told them it was their duty to eat, sleep and drink football. They should never worry about the opposition, that has always been my headache. It usually works, because players like a shoulder to cry on, they want someone to blame if things go wrong and, above all, they need someone to respect.

Orient will always have a place in my heart. It was my first job in League football and the first time I had built a club up and given them a bit of success. The fact that I went back twice more to team up with the club, and chairman Harry Zussman, only proves that, for a time, I couldn't live without them.

We were proud of our achievements; the players, staff and chairman could see things developing in front of their eyes. It was progress and surely that is what football management is all about. We used to make little chalk marks on the wall and say to ourselves, 'That is what we have achieved. That is all our own work.' It was a good feeling. And it was a good feeling to sign and work with players like Dennis Pacey, Vic Groves, Stan Charlton, Tom Johnstone, Phil Woosnam, Len Julians and Dave Sexton.

There was never any money at Orient to compete in the transfer market with the bigger clubs. You had to make sure your choice of player was right. There was just no allowance for failure. I remember following the performances of Groves for a long time before deciding it was time to strike. So one day I nipped off to Hackney where Groves worked in a Pie and Mash shop. I found him carrying boxes of eels and pickles around in the basement and asked the obvious question: 'Do you fancy giving this up and coming to play football?' He couldn't sign quickly enough and I had made one of my best signings. If you are chasing, you have got to chase hard.

It was a good atmosphere, and when I left Orient for short spells with Arsenal and with the Italian club Roma, I missed the worries of Orient. I missed the day-to-day problems that screamed at you every time you walked through the door.

I turned down many top jobs while at Orient, including Liverpool and Middlesbrough, and Harry Zussman had it about right when he said: 'Of course Alec had to consider offers and take these two jobs, but he has got a board here who give him complete control and good players. What more could a manager want?' And when I returned from Highbury after just fifty-three days, Harry paid me this wonderful compliment: 'Arsenal could do without Alec, we couldn't.'

Zussman was a happy man, a character who loved every minute of winning and said nothing when we lost. He just stayed out of the way and allowed his staff to put things right. He owned a Shoreditch shoe factory that specialized in ladies shoes and he had contacts and friends all over the country. I once sent Harry and my chief scout Sid Hobbins up to Blackburn to spy on a player, only for Hobbins to return in a furious mood. 'Alec, never send me on a job again with the chairman,' he said to me. 'He had so many contacts to visit we got there at half-time and had to leave before the end to catch the train home.'

I am delighted to say that apart from building a good side we managed to give Orient the success the club deserved. In 1952 we got to the fifth round of the FA Cup, beating Wrexham, Everton and Birmingham, before Arsenal beat us 3-0 and went on to reach the final.

Then, in 1956, we were promoted to Division Two after winning the old Division Three (South) by one point from Brighton. I am very proud of my promotion record throughout my career and if there had always been three up and three down as there is today I would have won promotion nine times. Sadly, the only club I failed to take 'up' was Fulham.

My love affair with Orient ended for the third and last time in March 1959 and this time there was no going back. For the first time I was confronted by a split board, people started to make decisions without consulting me. And as I have already explained, when directors start running the team that's the time to get out.

Three months later I joined Queen's Park Rangers. It had been a tough baptism and I crossed a lot of bridges at Yeovil and Orient. It was, however, the kind of grounding that I'm certain managers must get if they are to reach any kind of level in one of the toughest professions. Too many managers today are jumping into the Second Division without knowing what the life is really all about.

Having walked out on Arsenal and been, I thought, betrayed and double-crossed at Roma I didn't quite know what to expect at Queen's Park Rangers....

4 What is a Manager?

I have been interviewed by many chairmen in thirty-five years, accepted ten jobs, and turned down just as many. Yet not once have I been told exactly what my target, aim or job is. The interviews have been quick and simple: 'Hello Alec, would you like to come and manage the club?' 'Yes' 'Good, when can you start?' 'Tomorrow' 'Great'.

Every time I sign a contract or shake hands on a new job I have asked myself the same questions. What is a football manager, what is his role, how do you define a manager's job? Who am I?

They are intriguing questions and ninety-two Football League chairmen would probably all answer them differently. It is a job that needs no real qualifications, except of course experience. It is a career that could easily leave you a failure, an occupation that takes its toll on your health and family life.

The chairman, understandably, believes he is signing success every time he changes his manager. He is either backing his judgment, signing you on recommendation, or the success of a manager has persuaded him to pay a big compensation fee to another club. And yet there are no real guidelines, no hard-and-fast rules of the job. It is the man the club is signing, and the moment he puts pen to paper it is up to him to decide how he goes about it. How he brings the success is in his hands. But his own future is in the chairman's hands.

The wording of the contract is just as vague and this extract from my last contract as a manager, with Bournemouth, only proves what I am trying to say. It read:

> The Manager shall during his engagement with the club (subject at all times to the direction and control of the Board of Directors of the Club) have and exercise all the powers and discretions usually had and exercised by and perform do and carry out all duties acts matters and things usually performed done and carried out by a Manager of a Professional Football Club and in particular shall
>
> (a) Superintend direct and have control over trainers (who shall be selected by the Manager) groundsmen and football staff engaged by the club.
>
> (b) Generally to assist the Club in the procuration of players and to superintend the training employment and recreation of the players engaged by the club and to take all necessary and usual steps (including the selection of the players to be included in the club teams) to ensure that the Club teams shall appear at full strength and properly equipped at all matches in which they shall be engaged.

The phrase 'and carry out all duties acts matters and things usually performed done and carried out by a Manager of a Professional Football Club' underlines my point. I'm sure no one really knows how to describe us. There are, in fact, too many loopholes left gaping in a manager's contract and it is something that the authorities are looking into.

Why should men who have devoted years of their life to one club, and built up a successful business, suddenly be told to go, and be left with nothing? It is scandalous the way my profession is treated; it certainly would not happen in any other business. In another profession even the achievements of so-called 'failures' would carry them through for the rest of their lives.

I have always put fair play at the top of my list of qualities needed to run a club. To treat players fairly and to run the club fairly is not a bad motto. Mind you, being fair with players generally means giving them more money than the club can afford. That does allow you to demand value for money though – it means you can kick a few backsides and say 'Hey, you owe me, I owe you nothing'. You are looking for some sweat and application in return. It has certainly worked for me and I would put fairness as my recipe for success.

I have had many rows, of course, but they have always been short-fused affairs and respect is often born out of that kind of fight. It is no good fiddling about with players, telling them lies and promising them things you know you can't fulfil. It is no good telling a player 'We are on our way to the First Division' when you are signing him for a Third Division Club on Third Division wages.

Discipline is a dirty word which I don't like to write in my rule book. Club rules are made whenever I take control and if a player can't live with them he has no part to play. One day he will find himself quietly slipped out of the club. No fuss, no tantrums. Anyway, it has got to be a pretty shabby kind of bloke who can't do as he is told. If a manager says, 'be at the training ground at ten o'clock', why turn up at ten past? I have not been one for handing out fines either. I have told the players straight what I expect and, luckily, I haven't had much trouble.

I was let down once by a player called Jimmy Dunne while Fulham were in Hull for a Second Division match. Most players like to be tucked up in bed at a reasonable hour before a game but this lad was different on this occasion. He decided to have a night out and I sat waiting for him to return. When it got to two in the morning I noticed Dunne creeping back in and our eyes met. But instead of coming up to face me he tried to slide in through the kitchen and that, for me, made things worse.

If he had been a man and had faced me we could have had a row. I would have told him what I thought of him, and probably it would all have been forgotten. I didn't like him trying to hide and so Jimmy Dunne was sacked and transferred back to Torquay a few weeks later. It disappointed me to do it but I had been hurt.

Another so-called 'problem boy' I had under my control was Graham French, a superb winger in the Luton side which almost got to the First Division. Everyone knows now that French ended up in prison but to me he was a delight to handle and gave me absolutely no trouble. We used to talk for hours and I didn't pretend his behaviour outside football was brilliant white. I would just say: 'Look, I know all about you, tell me about it!' Perhaps that was French's problem, he didn't have enough people to listen to his worries.

The one thing I know is that I never replaced French in my Luton side. I signed David Court from Arsenal and that proved a bad buy. He wasn't the answer. I still think about French a lot and dream of what a great player he could have become, without his outside distractions.

I suppose I am lucky that most of my players have responded to my way of management. I used to stick a little sign up in the dressing room that read, 'When we train, we train. When we play, we play. And when we stop and have a beer, we will be bloody good at that too!'

Management today, of course, is far tougher because there are so many more problems to solve and Freedom of Contract is the biggest. Many years ago I stood up at a dinner and said that Freedom of Contract would destroy management and in a way it has. Players have become financially independent of you, men who are earning £1000 a week are no longer in a hurry to sign for a club. Suddenly it is the manager who is dashing to complete the deal. Bill Nicholson, the former Spurs manager and one of the 'greats' in my book, got it about right recently when he told me: 'Players were always in control but it is only now that they have realized it.'

Keith Burkinshaw, the Tottenham manager, went through weeks of torment in the summer of 1981 waiting for Glenn Hoddle, his brilliant England International star, to sign a new contract. Hoddle was in no hurry to sign because Freedom of Contract gave him licence to wait, the freedom to wait for another club to make him a better offer. And where did that leave Burkinshaw; right in the middle of team building for the next season? He didn't want to lose Hoddle and what is the good of £800,000 when you can't find a replacement in the same class? You can't play football with pound notes.

Twenty years ago I could have signed my entire first team squad in two hours. Today players come to sign contracts with their solicitors, accountants, shop stewards; you name them – I have negotiated with them. You say to the player, 'that's our wage structure,' and they look at you as if you are mad; they want you to smash it for them.

Then at the bottom end of the negotiating table, in the Third and Fourth Division, a player will ask to think the deal over. What he is really saying is 'I'm not signing for you'. What these players have got to realize is that if you break a wage structure for one man then the manager is under tremendous pressure to do it for others.

It is that kind of thing which often produces cracks in football clubs, little holes that become too wide to repair unless the management is strong and the organization behind the scenes is good. There is only one thing that covers up the cracks and that is winning, but only a few men and few clubs can win and that, I'm afraid, is what produces frightened management. Consequently they lose their jobs. It is a pressurised rat race, there is no doubt about that.

I have lived with, and like to think coped with, the pressure. I have always tried to wrestle any problems away from the players, a man can't give his best if he is worried about money, or something going on in the club he doesn't understand. All my players have been told 'Leave your problems in my office because I'm bloody good at worrying, in fact I'm an expert'. There are degrees of worry of course and when a player comes to see me with something on his mind I ask him 'Are your wife and kids OK?'. If the answer is yes then I tell him he hasn't really got any worries at all, only a few little problems to sort out.

Players are beginning to frighten me, however. I'm worried that the money they earn today has made them independent of effort. I have a little saying that 'Rich men don't sweat' and in some cases I'm positive this applies to some of our so-called top stars. Do they think: 'I have got a few bob in the bank, my pension scheme is growing, why should I do more than I have to?' I suppose, in the back of my mind, that is my little worry for the future of the game. Are we taking the incentive away from too many players? Are they becoming financially independent too early for their own and the game's good?

If you are an old 'worryguts' like me there are times when you think a football club is running too smoothly, everything is going too well. Many times at Queen's Park Rangers and Luton I used to watch the players in training at the end of the week and think to myself 'We have brought these up well, there is not much more we can teach them.'

You start to discuss a tactic with them and someone shouts 'OK Alec, we know, leave this to us.' You begin to think you are out of work, you are just a backroom boy.

It doesn't help when your secretary asks if you have picked the team. 'Is it the same as last week?' she asks. 'Yes'. 'I thought it was' she adds. 'I have typed it out already. Who is the sub ... Jim Smith? Oh good, I have put him in as well.' She had picked the team, everything was going so well that my life was easy. All I had to do was finish my coffee, walk a few yards and pin the team sheet up on the wall.

But that's not me, I like to worry. My wife will confirm that there haven't been many days gone by without my worrying about something. When I was out of work I used to get under her feet, the grass would be cut and roses pruned by 11 o'clock in the morning. 'For God's sake Alec,' she would say, 'Go out, do something'.

Football has been my life and I have not been happy unless I have been involved with football people. Marjorie has been a wonderful wife, the backbone of the Stock family and a great support to me in my job. She knows more about football than any other women I know and has ate, slept and drank soccer with me for long periods. Many occasions I have said to her, 'Come on, luv, I'll take you out for a meal', and she will look disappointed and say 'You know that Wimbledon Reserves are playing.'

My daughters too have been involved although the Rangers sacking affected them all and their enthusiasm was never really the same again. Marjorie bombed up to Luton from time to time in her white Mini but it wasn't the same for her. But I have been very lucky.

She has also understood me, which is a necessity for any football marriage. She knows the hours are unpredictable and yet has never really complained, never thrown a tantrum when the phone has rung after she has changed and is ready to go out for the evening. 'Sorry luv' I would say. 'I'm going to be late again.' There have been many of those phone calls, many times when Marjorie has had to change her plans at the eleventh hour. I just wish some of football's directors were as understanding as she is.

I wish when directors were sacking a manager they would stop and ask themselves: 'Should we just kick this bloke out in the street. Hasn't he worked round the clock for us seven days a week, hasn't he built up our youth policy, brought us success over the years, got home in the early hours of the morning after a spying journey to the other end of the country and still been in for training, hasn't he produced some superb players for us, hasn't he done all we wanted until the last few weeks? Should we really be treating him like this?' I wish that is what they would think, but most of them never do.

Although I have always had confidence in my ability, and knew from the first months at Yeovil that I had a lot to offer management, I often wish I had been more self-assured throughout my career. My ego has never pushed me on. I should, I suppose, have accepted one or two of the top jobs I was offered but I have always wanted to do my own thing. When I look back I have no doubt that I achieved immense enjoyment from taking Orient, Rangers, Luton and Fulham and giving them a little bit of success they perhaps didn't expect.

I can also definitely say that if I could turn back the clock I would pick a career in management again. I would not necessarily do all the same things but, yes, I would be a manager. There are regrets, of course, and yet Football League managers belong to an exclusive club; there are only ninety-two of us and I am very proud to have been around for so long.

My regrets are not many and I suppose the biggest must have been my handling of the Arsenal situation, something that I will explain later in the book. I have always regretted selling good players but that is something in football that managers can't always control. I know now I should have promoted Ken Craggs at Fulham instead of calling in Bobby Campbell as my number two. And I'm sure it was a mistake to go back to Queen's Park Rangers as a director when the Fulham bust-up was at its peak.

But when Fulham were talking of making me a consultant and Jim Gregory rang to ask if I would like to return as a director it seemed a good idea at the time. I could tell Fulham what to do with their consultancy. It was a big and brave decision because I walked out on a Testimonial at Craven Cottage. Now, however, I'm sure that Jim asked me back to clear his conscience from all those years before. I was grateful of course but it was probably the wrong decision. Jim even put me in temporary charge of the team during a period when Frank Sibley resigned.

And yet now I wonder whether, if Jim had found me more to do, I would have ended my career at Bournemouth. Don't get me wrong, I am happy at Bournemouth and the chairman Harold Walker is a fine man to work for, but perhaps I miss London a little bit. Sometimes I miss being involved with the London scene, the telephone calls, people dropping in; there is certainly no doubt in my mind that London is the place to be if you are involved with football.

I still do my dreaming. Gardening is my hobby and I lose myself in the garden for hours digging and tending to my vegetable patch. I dream of becoming the oldest man to win the League Cup and FA Cup ... it is only a dream, of course.

Management is all about having good players around you

and doing and saying the right things at the right time. A favourite little story of mine that has always hung in my memory took place at Orient after the last League game of the season and when most of the professional staff had 'signed off' for the summer. I had let them go even though we had a Mid-Week League match against Watford to fulfil.

I only had the reserve goalkeeper and apprentice centre half as obvious choices and so the rest of the side was patched up with whoever was available. The assistant secretary played, I turned out at right back, one of the backroom boys, Jimmy Richardson (remembered as the Newcastle player who pulled the ball back from behind the by-line in the famous Cup Final incident against Arsenal) came out of retirement. And a young local reporter called Peter Lorenzo pulled on the number seven shirt.

It didn't matter because I knew that Watford wouldn't take it too seriously, they would just want to get the fixture out the way and, like us, their season finished. To my horror they turned up with their first team and Tony Collins, a very talented left winger, gave me the run-around and at half time we were 0-5 down.

During the interval we were a shambles, sitting around in a heap and it didn't help when someone came in to tell me that the Watford manager was boasting that his team were about to get double figures and break the Mid-Week League scoring record.

'OK lads' I said immediately. 'We might have to fight this one out.' I didn't know what we were quite going to fight with but within minutes of the re-start I had picked a verbal fight with their left half and captain, just to liven our team up you understand, and for some reason things started to improve. I don't know whether my half-time battle cry worked or my decision to pick a fight got through but I like to think what followed represented a little victory for man-management.

We scored to make it 5-1 and began to play better. Suddenly it was 5-3, only for Watford to make it 6-3. Back we came and then Lorenzo completed a superb hat-trick to reduce their lead to just one goal. The few people inside the ground had even begun to take an interest and when Richardson scored to equalize at 6-6 with one of his left-footed specials there was even a roar.

Watford were now in total disarray, fighting and arguing between themselves and when four defenders stood and watched our seventh goal trickle in I couldn't help taking a look at their manager. 'Who's going into the record books now.' In the last minute Collins jinked his way past me and two others into the area and slipped through a ball that their centre forward couldn't miss. To complete an amazing afternoon our centre half dived on the ball. It was an obvious penalty, or was it?

The referee, God bless him, had clearly got involved with the strange goings-on of that afternoon at Leyton Stadium. I can see him now, turning to the Watford players and saying: 'Lads, I have been a referee for many years and have seen an awful lot of things on this pitch this afternoon that I never expected to witness. If you think I am going to give a penalty now you have got another think coming.' And with that he picked up the ball and blew his whistle ... we had won.

I can remember that match as if it was yesterday, I can still see the faces of my players in the dressing-room afterwards. Who can tell if that turn-round had anything to do with me? Did those players really respond to their manager? Who knows? But that is management, why do players respond to one man and not the other. What makes a cracking manager?

My favourite manager has always been Bill Nicholson. Bill had dignity, a little something about him that the players respected and, above all, he was a winner. Everything purred about Nicholson's Tottenham team and it was the way he won, the kind of football his teams played. Any manager who has been a five out of five Wembley winner deserves a place in football history.

There was never any jealousy towards Spurs because Bill had done everything so well. When you set out on a Saturday morning for your game you would always think 'I hope Old Bill wins today, I hope Spurs turn it on.' There was no envy because it was good for the game that a team like Spurs, and a man like Nicholson, stayed at the top.

Every manager when he sets out wants to write a little piece of history for himself, he wants to leave his stamp on the game. Tactically there have been three great achievements. Herbert Chapman gave us the stopper centre half and that has stuck. Arthur Rowe invented the lovely push and run side and then came Sir Alf Ramsey's wingless wonders. Those systems have stayed with us and what a marvellous feeling to sit back and say at the end of your day, 'I invented that, it's my own contribution to the development of this great game'. Many people will argue that Ramsey did the game a great disservice when he won the World Cup with his wingless wonders. My answer to them is that he did it, he won, he made the system work.

Hungary offered us the deep-lying centre forward and for a long time we saw number nines in deep positions, playing behind their own forward line. One day someone somewhere discovered that our friend playing almost in his own half was not a danger so he was just given the ball. It was discovered that he was only a threat if you started to try and stop him play. So that system was defeated.

We come then to the managers who are winners, not the men who have flashed in and out for the occasional trophy but the managers who have won on a regular basis. The men who have stayed at the top in their own era. Managers like Sir Matt Busby, Bill Shankly, Nicholson, Ramsey, Don Revie and today Bob Paisley and Brian Clough. There is no substitute for winning and these men have won more than most. They have had players and teams who excite you.

Take Bob Paisley. Who thought he could follow Shankly at Liverpool so superbly and now Bob goes down as the most successful manager in English football history. He has done something that no one could possibly have dreamt an English manager would do and that is win the European Cup three times. And I bet he hasn't finished yet.

Brian Clough too is way up there for building two

Championship sides from nothing at Derby and Nottingham Forest and winning the European Cup twice. They are record breakers.

Their buying and developing too is fantastic. I'm not talking about big money signings. I'm sure it was far easier for Cloughie to sign Peter Shilton than find Roy McFarland and build him up into an England International. Yet that is what Clough does time and time again, pick a player out of obscurity, wave a magic wand and, hey presto, he is a big star. There is only one thing left for one of these managers to win now and that is the treble, and who would bet against Clough or Paisley being first to achieve that.

And yet despite the great men and the great knowledge we have in this country, I fear that the top brass looks down on managers. They don't seem to want to accept us, or involve us in any future planning the game needs. They certainly don't recognize – as I do – that managers are the most important people in the game.

If you got us all together once in a while I'm sure, in fact I know, that we might just put football dead right. We might just come up with the answers. It seems incredible to me that so much knowledge can be wasted when the game has reached the crossroads and everyone is crying out for solutions and new ideas. How can people like Ramsey, Busby, Nicholson, Joe Mercer, Rowe, Shankly, me if you like, and many more, just be lost to the game?

We have no House of Lords to speak at and yet there should be somewhere to go where we can voice opinions and offer constructive arguments. It is a travesty that people who are in authority at one moment can be pushed aside and forgotten the next. It could only happen in football.

And why does it happen? Is it because there are too many people sitting on committees and in nice little jobs who might just have to move over? Are they people who stick knives in managers' backs the moment they see their little world in danger? Referees have meetings and discussions, coaches go away on courses and meet up, and where do managers go ... on the scrapheap, forgotten.

Football has been crying out for years for a better relationship between players and referees. Why isn't there then a monthly meeting between managers and referees, why can't the gap be closed and the problems be ironed out? There must be someone somewhere with a cracking job who doesn't allow meetings like that. Is he one of the backroom men who doesn't want change, one of the men who are scared that once people who know start making changes their lives will never be the same again?

Management is a very lonely job. You know that after a few bad results your head will be on the chopping block. But your pride stops you from screaming. You just keep slogging away and hope that the miracle will happen, and praying that your chairman has got a bit of style and will support you.

It was good to hear Bobby Robson of Ipswich talking when he was linked with Sunderland during the 1981 summer. He said that if he ever left Ipswich he would want a ten-year contract. 'That's how long it takes to get a club how you want it, that's how long it takes to get it running really smoothly', he said. 'I don't want someone saying to me after three years that we haven't won anything and you have got to go.' Perhaps at last we are waking up to the fact that managers have been trodden on and treated badly for too long.

I hope in another thirty-five years someone else will stand up and say, 'Gentlemen, the average life of a manager at one club is now ten years.' At last the question, what is a manager, would have been answered.

5 A Day in the Life . . .

I will remember Saturday 11 May 1968 as long as I live. The longest day in my life is etched on my memory, engraved there so I can never forget the nightmare pressure of that afternoon at Villa Park in front of a capacity crowd.

When people talk about pressure and tension in football I hope the following story proves that it is there. It was a feeling of complete helplessness for me as I sat on a bench on the edge of the pitch and watched my Queen's Park Rangers team battle for the victory that meant so much to us all – the win that would take us into the First Division.

It was the match I had waited for ever since I came into management. There was no turning back; the players and I had travelled a long way together and to fail on the last day of the season would have been nothing short of disastrous. It was also my chance to equal the record held by Jimmy Seed, the proud record of taking a team from the Third to the First Division in successive seasons, a day that would never come round again.

It is difficult to put into words exactly how I felt when I sat down just before three o'clock. It was the climax of twenty-one years in management and nine long hard months of that season when I had struggled a lot with asthma. And they certainly took me to the summit of anxiety. In the end that day reached its climax in three minutes of torture, three minutes when my body was drained of every drop of feeling. I was left completely numb ... they talk about pressure!

You often hear managers saying that they have no power over what goes on after their players have left the dressing room. And that is how I felt. The coaching staff and I had built them up, persuaded them, loved them, done everything to get them in the right frame of mind. In the end the last instruction was simple: 'If we beat Aston Villa we will be in the First Division next season.'

So out they went, my team, the side that had been built carefully, a group of players certainly good enough to do well in the top drawer. It's a team that will always roll off my tongue. Mike Kelly; Ian Watson, Alan Harris; Mike Keen, Bobby Keetch, Tony Hazell; Ian Morgan, Mick Leach, Frank Clarke, Rodney Marsh, Les Allen.

We had already performed a little miracle earlier that season and certainly I had my doubts about promotion before the first kick when the side was devastated by injury. I had written off Rodney Marsh for weeks with a bone graft in his leg and when Ron Hunt collided with a cameraman during a friendly at Southend he was out for three months.

I had arranged another friendly fixture before the season with the Italian Under-23 side – a team brought over to England by Gigi Peronace, a lovely man who died suddenly and tragically at the end of 1980 – when sure enough our injury jinx struck again. This time it was winger Roger Morgan, who damaged a leg, and he too was missing when we began. Then, on the Monday before the first match, Keith Sanderson, our amateur inside forward and a very vital member of the team, was injured in a friendly at Brentford. So within a couple of weeks all my planning for the start of the season had been ruined.

Back we go to the question 'What is a manager?' On this occasion a manager was a man who felt like crying and telling the world that everything and everyone was against him. Instead he had to hide his bitter frustration, keep the morale of the entire staff sky high and, most importantly, find some players from somewhere.

We called up a couple of kids called Dave Clement and Micky Leach, introduced a boy called Alan Wilks, a free signing from Chelsea, and asked the old man, former Fulham full back Jim Langley, to help hold things together at the back. It was a strange old side I pinned up for that first game in the Second Division but my worries soon evaporated into relief as we took eleven points out of twelve. It was the platform we needed and from then on we seemed a fair bet for promotion.

In the run-in to that last vital Saturday, Ipswich, under Bill McGarry, were the leaders and we were never far behind. But then Blackpool threw a spanner in the works by winning their last seven matches before the nail-biting day. And so we went into the final match of the season needing to win to go up. It couldn't have been closer; Ipswich had 57 points from 41 matches and Blackpool, who were away to Huddersfield, had 56 points. We had 56 points too but our goal average was superior. Ipswich, of course, couldn't afford to slip either. They knew that if they lost and we and Blackpool both won, they would be pipped at the last fence. It was a marvellous occasion for the fans and the media but one that puts years on a manager.

Marjorie knew how I would be feeling on that Saturday morning. She understood the pressure, and the girls, Sarah and Elizabeth, were given due warning before I came down for breakfast. 'One word out of place' she told them, 'and he will bite your heads off. Just eat up and quietly go.'

I have always been a superstitious person and am a great believer in using the same routine when you are worried about something. So when I left home at 9.30 in the morning I was wearing the same suit, shirt and blue socks I had worn on match days throughout that season. Marjorie had said 'Good luck' by the front door and for some reason that shook me. 'Why should I need luck?' I said to myself. 'No one can help me and I don't need luck, we damn well deserve to go up.'

The coach was waiting at Shepherds Bush and I ordered the driver to use exactly the same route he had always taken to Villa Park. It sounds stupid now but for some reason I thought it was the right thing to do, I just had a feeling we shouldn't change our habit.

As I sat on the coach in the same seat I always used I went through every game we had played that season, tossing over in my mind just how we were going to play that afternoon and I always came back with the same opinion, Aston Villa couldn't beat us ... could they?

I would never have admitted it to anyone else on that coach but I knew I was nervous. The occasion had got to me and as we neared the Midlands the chewed up feeling in my stomach only got worse. So I stuck my hands deep in my pockets to hide my nervousness (an old Army dodge) and pretended to go to sleep.

As we were passing through Newport Pagnell I suddenly began to think of the referee Leo Callaghan, a solid honest man. I hoped he knew just how much the game meant to me. I remembered the last time he had controlled one of our games at Loftus Road and how well we looked after him. 'I hope he remembers those sandwiches we had that day' I thought to myself. 'They were a bit special and Leo commented on them.' I began to get quite neurotic about Callaghan and the sandwiches we had given him for his after-match snack. 'Remember those sandwiches Leo' I kept saying to myself. 'Remember those bloody sandwiches.'

At Villa Park the tension was unbearable and all I wanted to do was get the game over and return quickly to my four walls at Epsom. It was a nightmare. At half-time and after the longest forty-five minutes of my life Aston Villa were winning 1-0 and we had played badly, full of nerves; just like I felt. I didn't know the Blackpool score and as I walked towards our dressing-room I remember thinking, 'I never want to go through this kind of day again'.

We were immediately lifted in the second half by an equalizing goal from Mick Leach. It was what we wanted and promotion was in the air again, as long as Blackpool were not winning. The nightmare blew up in my face once more when a girl fan dressed from head to toe in the blue and white colours of Queen's Park Rangers tapped me on the shoulder. She was holding a radio to her ear and shouted 'Mr Stock, Blackpool have just scored at Huddersfield!' It was the kind of news I could have done without, especially in my nervous state, and she really became my favourite lady a few minutes later when she announced that Blackpool were two up.

I did everything I could to lift the players from then on, shouting and screaming, jumping up and down, pointing, encouraging, criticizing – but with fifteen minutes left I had nothing more to offer. I had run out of everything, including steam and prayers, and I could see my dream disappearing.

Then, with four minutes left, Rodney Marsh chased a long through-ball into the Villa box. He couldn't reach it to get in a shot but pressurized their full back Keith Bradley so much that he pushed the ball wide of his goalkeeper. An own goal, we were ahead with an own goal!

I screamed at Bill Dodgin to find out how long to go. 'Three minutes, Boss' he said. Three minutes. How could they do this to me. I was up on my feet again and this time the only person I could think of was the referee. 'Leo' I screamed. 'Blow the whistle you Welsh bastard. This means a lot to me. Come on, it's time!' knowing full well there were still two minutes left. Callaghan had to stop the game and ordered me to calm down but it wasn't easy.

There were about thirty seconds to go when Aston Villa were given a free kick just inside our half and, of course, they ordered everyone into our penalty box. As the kick dropped towards our goal all I could see was a mass of claret and blue shirts pouring in on the goal. It was like the charge of the light brigade and I could hardly bear to watch. 'Christ,' I thought 'They are going to score.'

Then it happened, dear, dear Leo Callaghan ... he *did* remember those sandwiches ... and blew the final whistle. We were up, we had reached the First Division.

Everyone in the dressing-room afterwards was shattered. The match had taken a lot out of us all and as you can imagine I was a wreck, drained of everything except happiness. Marshy wanted to claim the goal and I was revived by the champagne that had arrived. I was handed a big enamel cup full of bubbly and it didn't matter that there were tea leaves floating on the top. It was the sweetest drink of them all. It tasted of winning and achievement.

It had been so close that many miles away in Huddersfield, Blackpool had also got the champagne out. They thought we had only drawn and they were in the First Division. I knew on the happy journey home that there could never be another situation like that for me. It was Roy of the Rovers, now or never stuff, and who can argue that being a manager during matches is not full of tension and pressure.

I watched with sympathy the 1981 League Cup Final when West Ham manager John Lyall and referee Clive Thomas argued after the final whistle. How is a manager supposed to remain calm when, seconds earlier, he has seen something snatched from his club in a controversial fashion?

I was still on cloud nine the next morning, reading the Sunday newspapers and answering many phone calls of congratulation, when my eldest daughter Elizabeth brought me down to earth. 'Daddy' she said. 'I don't mind you swearing but when I can hear you above 40,000 people and across the other side of the pitch I find it most undignified!'

Nothing, however, could have upset me that Sunday morning. I was relaxed and happy and wouldn't have dreamt that in seven months I would be sacked and that the following season my Queen's Park Rangers team would go straight back down again with just 18 points from their 42 matches.

While I was convalescing and waiting for Jim Gregory to call me back to work I often watched QPR matches. What I saw I couldn't believe and on 30 September 1968, with the team anchored to the bottom of the First Division without a victory, I sent the chairman a report. He didn't ask for it but there were so many things wrong I thought someone should bring them to the attention of the board.

My sacking a few weeks later shocked a lot of people and some directors and many friends wrote to me telling me of their sadness. They weren't half as sad as I was, leaving that team behind. The last time I worked with those players was in that Villa Park dressing-room ... on the longest day of my life.

6 Corruption

I thought that after thirty-five years in management I was past being shocked. I thought I had seen the lot, good and bad players, straight and dishonest chairmen and directors. Situations that have made me cry one minute and then dance with joy the next. I accept them all as part of a manager's life, part of a profession that is like no other.

I have been sacked and kicked in the teeth, have resigned and regretted it, sold players I loved, signed others I didn't want. I have been double-crossed, asked for money by players that I knew my club couldn't afford and seen football change so much in the last ten years that I fear and wonder what is going to happen to the game.

It seems, however, that there is more to learn, even at my age. There are things going on in football that I didn't dream existed, things I just don't want to be associated with. And yet things I can't avoid.

And, yes, I have been shocked by allegations and rumours that bring a nasty taste to my mouth and something that can only throw management into the gutter and send it gurgling down the drain, unless it is stamped out immediately. I have been shocked by allegations of. corruption in football management.

Maybe I am old-fashioned in my outlook and upbringing, perhaps a strict Army background didn't create enough bad in me. But corruption is something I don't want to know about, especially when, indirectly, it affects me. I am a proud old professional and when something like this happens to my profession I fight and hit back like mad.

As soon as I heard the rumours I rushed for my dictionary and the definition of corruption is 'to pervert, to make evil and bribe'. Never in my life did I think I would know the day when those things were said about a sport and profession I love. That is why I have decided to bring the whole thing out into the open and try and rescue the image of management and prove that, surely, it is only directed at a few.

I am not naïve enough not to realize that clubs are under tremendous pressure to break the law and give players big underhand payments as an incentive to sign for them. There are certain clubs who do this openly and have a reputation throughout football. Players get to know this and their demands are high. It is a form of football blackmail. But I never dreamt that managers were now making the same demands.

I suppose at the back of my mind the rumours have always been there and, without consciously thinking about it, I have turned my mind off completely. It came up and hit me in the face however during the 1981 season when the phone rang at my Bournemouth home. It was a woman reporter from one of our top newspapers and she wanted to come and see me to do an article. 'Lovely' I said. 'Come down whenever you like.'

It was obvious from the word go when she arrived that she knew nothing about sport and was from the news side. 'I am on an investigation team and we are trying to blow corruption in football open. We want you to talk about corruption in management.'

I presume she came to me as one of the old boys, someone who had seen everything. I expect they said to themselves 'Go and see Alec Stock, he has been around for years, he must know all about this.' Well, I must have been a big disappointment to that girl reporter because I couldn't tell her a thing. I just sat her down and said 'Darling, you are on virgin soil, you tell me. Go on, fill me in.'

It was a very enlightening discussion. She talked about

clubs, chairmen, players and managers. She wanted leads but I couldn't give them to her.

It is said that managers are demanding kick-backs of their own on transfers, especially on foreign deals. On one hand you have got the player demanding an under-the-counter payment for signing and on the other the manager is saying 'You can't have him unless there is something in it for me. If there is nothing in it for me, no deal.' Well, in my book that stinks, it is the most wicked thing I have heard in the job.

Yet when I ask around and talk to friends in football the rumours are there, they have been there apparently for a long time. So I can only presume that the allegations might be true. As a very proud manager I like to think that these are only rumours and allegations. I must and will always have great faith in my profession until someone shows me concrete evidence to prove me wrong.

The allegations are getting too close for comfort, however, and that is why I have written this chapter. I want it to act as a warning. I have decided to bring it out into the open. I can't name names because how do you prove something like this? But the managers it does concern – and I pray and hope it's only a few – be warned. People are looking for you, people in authority inside and outside the game realize what is going on and will blow it sky high given the chance.

I never thought the day would come when someone knocked on my door and talked about corruption. It is something I don't want. I felt like running away, because corruption, in my book, is something you can go inside for. As I care so much I have thought long and hard about this subject. I have gone back over my career many times, searching for the phone call and conversation that should have opened my eyes to what was going on.

I must say I have never thought there was anything wrong with a manager who is rewarded for doing a good bit of business for his club. This happened to me when I was at Luton when I signed Malcolm Macdonald for £17,500 and eventually sold him to Newcastle for £180,000. The club was clearly happy with the deal, especially as I had upped the price by £30,000 overnight, and they gave me a bonus. That, I believe, is part and parcel of everyday business, a financial reward for doing a good job. Today, however, there are even stories of managers having written agreements giving them a cut of players' transfer fees.

Even in Italy I didn't smell this ugly word called corruption. We had a fella, a sort of in-between man, who did the negotiating and signing of new players and I just took it for granted that he was probably making a few bob out of the deals he was doing. I had no evidence but that is what everyone seemed to accept. I often thought 'What a bloody good job that fella has got, dashing all over the world and signing players.' When you have got players coming in from Europe and America the transfers have to be expertly handled and, yes, I thought – perhaps a 'few things were going on.'

But it certainly never filtered through to me and I was never approached or asked. I had my doubts, because it was Italy. But I never brought those doubts back to England when I returned.

The job has always been the same to me. Working away to improve the team and consequently the club, doing things in an orderly, above-board fashion. I have signed and sold more players than most but the word 'fiddle' never came into conversations I have had with other managers.

Yet now you hear fans and even people inside the game saying 'I bet so and so made a few bob out of that' or 'How much did he ask for?' It is a very sad part of life, we have all become far too cynical.

Managers I have known and respected have always had to fight off the player who held clubs to ransom, the guy who suddenly demands a backhander. At my end of the tree the most I have been asked for is £2,000, although the cocky ones might try and squeeze you. I look at them through sad eyes. 'Son', I say, 'You are dreaming, I'm glad we haven't done a deal because I don't want you in my club.'

Can it also be right that players put themselves on the market just because they are hard up? For example, the man who has gambled his money away and needs help, who asks for a transfer and pays off his debts with the money he receives from his next club. That kind of player is on the market for one thing only, to make money.

Yet some clubs listen and even encourage it. If a player is undecided who to sign for, one club will let it be known that they will break the rules to get their man. Backhanders certainly didn't happen years ago and yet sadly today they are part and parcel of the inflated and complex transfer system.

The late Harry Zussman at Orient had a lovely saying: 'When you fiddle the tax man you have got to have a very long memory.' And he was right, why shouldn't players pay their own tax bills, everyone else does. Managers and clubs, of course, have only got themselves to blame if they become involved in these things. They are putting their reputations in the hands of other people. They may get away with it a few times but in the end they are found out, their reputation falls so low that they disappear from the game.

They are men who live under constant pressure. And the pressure becomes heavier after you have broken football law. He must ask himself thousands of times 'How reliable is that player? Will he announce to the world what my club has done?' If the player is unreliable and goes around blabbing, or when he leaves he puts the knife in, then you are in trouble.

If you do it for one you are under pressure to do it for others and soon you are known throughout football as the man who gives away a few bob. There is a queue outside your door of players who want a cut of the action and, right at the end of the queue, is the man in authority who has heard too. He wants to have a look at the books, he wants to know all about you. My message to these managers who break the rules and allow these things to happen at their clubs is simple. You are bloody fools.

The other manager who sickens me is the man who is always running to the press – usually for money – to voice off about someone else's team and players. To me, they are just as guilty. He will tell the paper: 'I will say what you like, you write it and I'll put my name to it. But how much?'

Don't those men realize that they are only killing their image and eating into the reputation of football. They haven't really got an opinion and the public reaction, in the end, is: 'Not him again!' He loses all credibility.

I once came out in very strong defence of Sir Alf Ramsey when the knives were out for the only man who won us the World Cup. He was having a terrible time in the press and even two of our then top managers, Malcolm Allison and Tommy Docherty, joined in the Ramsey baiting. I saw red then and hit back hard. They were damaging football's reputation.

This kind of man doesn't do it for the image of the game, he does it for hard cash and it is something that we can well and truly do without. As I have said I was delighted that in 1981 the nice guys won and kept out in front. The managers who don't criticize their fellow professionals, who don't bleat for the sake of it, got their reward.

Now the final insult to my profession is this allegation of corruption. Surely we can't stoop any lower. It is something that undermines football and eats away at the foundations that have taken so long to become established.

I certainly don't want to retire with this kind of smear spread across the face of football and I hope that, eventually, we can go back to good old-fashioned negotiation and not blackmail. Surely there is no need to act in this manner, top managers in the country are now being paid between £25,000 and £40,000 basic a year. Their future is secure without their stooping to demand underhand payments.

I must admit that if I had been told that corruption was spreading through directors I wouldn't have been surprised. I wouldn't put it past some I have known and worked with. But managers, that is different.

And while we worry about players and their demands, what chance have they got if some managers stink. How can we blame players? If managers are on the fiddle – and that is what I am saying – how can we look players in the face and say 'No'. If managers are in there shopping around then the game hasn't got a leg to stand on.

It is surely getting very close when this subject has got to be raised, discussed and minuted at a meeting of the Secretary and Managers Association. It is most likely that everyone would say 'Whoops' and put their heads down and sweep the entire thing under the carpet. But this is too dangerous to ignore.

At my age, and at this stage of my career, I suppose it shouldn't matter to me. Yet it matters even more because football management means a lot, it has been my life and I don't like to see the image that an awful lot of good blokes have worked for disappear.

We are only talking about a minority of men here but these fellas are spoiling it for others. Corruption must be stamped out and I hope by bringing this out into the open I can help kill it off. I like to think that the nice guys always win. In this case, they must.

7 Marsh and Macdonald

Rodney Marsh and Malcolm Macdonald represent what my career has been all about. The excitement and immense personal satisfaction of finding a rare talent, taking a gamble and turning that talent into something special; moulding and discovering an international star.

They are the two players who have given me my embarrassing reputation as the star maker, although there are other players, and club achievements, that have made me just as proud.

Marsh and Macdonald are certainly the biggest names. I signed Rodney from Fulham for £15,000 in March 1966 and Queen's Park Rangers eventually sold him to Manchester City for £200,000. Malcolm was a snip at £17,500, again from Fulham, and I reluctantly sold him to Newcastle for £180,000. You will agree, two very good bits of business.

It is no secret that I have always preferred London players. I know and trust them and feel happiest working with them. It is no coincidence either that Macdonald and Marsh were both signed from Fulham. As a manager I always used to wait for Fulham's retained players' list at the end of the season and go and buy one of the men they were letting go. I always thought that Fulham threw away bargains, they seemed to let talent and experience go for nothing, and people like Jim Langley, Bobby Keetch, Marsh and Macdonald have only proved me right.

Signing players is just a game of individual choice. You

can travel hundreds of miles one day because your scout in Newcastle thinks he has found the best new centre forward since Tommy Lawton; and you take one look at him and think 'No, this has been a wasted journey.'

All the time you are looking for the player who can turn your team into winners. It is difficult to explain what attracts you to a boy the country hasn't heard of, but one flash of inspiration, one shrug of the shoulders, one shot, one dribble, one pass can persuade you. You make a mental note and pray that no one else has seen the same things, no one else is about to outbid you. I have travelled thousands of miles in my career looking for players and yet I found my two jewels on the doorstep, under my nose at Craven Cottage.

I first saw Marsh play for Fulham reserves in a midweek match against Charlton. I hadn't gone to the game especially to see the kid with blond hair and high steps because if you were a London manager in those days you always turned up at Craven Cottage on a Wednesday afternoon. It was the place to go, it was a fun afternoon to break up the week.

All the local managers would shut up their own shop at lunchtime and go along to Fulham for a cup of tea and a chat. It was part of the 'London scene' and something that made Fulham a little bit special. You just enjoyed being there, it had that little ingredient of style. We didn't get much work done once we arrived at the ground because there was always someone to chat to, an old friend to reminisce with. And when the game started characters like Tosh Chamberlin on the left wing made sure everyone inside the ground was entertained.

On this particular occasion I had rung Fulham in the morning to ask them their team and thought about the players in their reserve side as I drove the few miles from Shepherds Bush. I thought about Marsh and couldn't understand why someone who had played in all but one League match the previous year was now in the reserves.

I knew he had made his debut for Fulham in 1963 and a year later had suffered an accident against Leicester that doctors thought should have ended his career. He collided with a goalpost, suffered concussion and from that day lost the hearing in his left ear. But here he was playing again and I wondered why he was not back in the first team.

I had heard he had fallen out with Fulham's manager Vic Buckingham and that they were not keen even to allow him to train with the other players. It certainly seemed a funny old set up although I didn't worry about it too much because this was Fulham on a Wednesday afternoon and that meant entertainment.

Sure enough Fulham didn't let us down and produced one of the funniest penalty incidents I have ever seen. They were awarded a spot kick during the second half and all the cabbies standing in the enclosure in front of the main stand called for the biggest goalkeeper you have ever seen, a giant South African called Hewkins, to come up and take it. In traditional music hall style he arrived and, to the delight of the hundred or so people watching, hit the bar.

He didn't just hit the bar, he almost bent it in half and the ball rebounded almost to the half-way line where four Charlton forwards gratefully scampered off to score, with Hewkins in desperate pursuit.

Throughout the game Marsh had been quiet compared with the other things going on. Yet I was impressed with his control and shooting, he had a certain arrogance that seemed to lift him above the rest of the players on view. Yes, I thought he was worth a gamble.

I spoke to my chairman Jim Gregory and he also liked what he saw. That was one of Gregory's strong points, if he agreed with you he would back you all the way and we signed Marsh for £15,000. I suppose we took a chance, because immediately he had signed there were people in the game who took great delight in telling us what was wrong with our new player. 'He is a clown' they said. 'He doesn't like hard work and he isn't consistent.'

I wasn't particularly looking for consistency, I wanted style and imagination. I wanted someone to bring something out of the Rangers team. I wasn't quite sure what but just had a feeling that Rodney Marsh had it in him to lift the players around him just by turning up. I thought he could be special.

Well, the worst thing happened and Rodney lived up to his description during his debut at Peterborough. He was awful. 'We are going to have to work damn hard with this one' I told my staff on the way back from the game. 'But mark my words it will be worth it.'

Sure enough after four days with him in training we began to see a different Marsh. Suddenly he lost his awkwardness and developed into a beautiful animal. For a big man Rod had a very delicate touch and he is still the only player I have seen who could dribble without looking at the ball. It was as if he had the ball tied to a piece of string and whatever you asked him to do he could do it.

He could chip goals from impossible angles, beat men with a swivel of his hips, climb higher than anyone else in the club, dribble through packed defences; you name it – Rodney would have a go and usually succeed. He could also argue with referees and linesmen and flare up when opponents got too rough; yes, there was always something happening when Marsh was playing.

It was the era of the twin centre forward and Marsh and Les Allen were our answer to Liverpool's Ian St John and Roger Hunt or Geoff Hurst and Johnny Byrne at West Ham. They were not only our match winners but they entertained too. The crowd loved Rodney and we gave them the eerie chant of 'Rod – nee, Rod – nee', something that has stuck ever since.

You even hear it at Test matches these days when Rodney's namesake is keeping wicket for Australia. The crowd love Rodney so much that once when he was suspended our average gate went down from 20,000 to 11,000, and they all came back the moment his ban was over.

He was my dream. I have always told players, first I want to win, then I want to win well and thirdly I want to win with a bit of character and style. Marsh gave Queen's Park Rangers all that, and more. I think he and I got on because I treated him fairly and like a man. The first time I met him I said 'Fulham say you are a clown, I hope you are not going to try and prove it for me.' He was always a bit outlandish but nothing bad and never took umbrage when we had our differences of opinion.

He had great presence and always seemed to be a bit of a loner, appeared to be aloof and on a different plane to everyone else. And yet underneath the surface he was just the same as everyone, a good old cockney kid. I remember the time he knocked on our door and asked Marjorie if she would rush his wife Jean into hospital as she had gone into labour for their first child. Rodney then squirmed around in the back seat of Marjorie's Mini, pleading with the rush hour traffic in Epsom to get out of the way. After the baby had arrived Rodney was a very proud father.

I would sometimes catch him walking around Epsom without shoes and socks on, four days growth on his chin and wearing a Barcelona number six shirt. He was showing off, of course, and I used to catch him up and tell him, 'You need a kick up the backside. You're a public figure, get dressed properly.' And Rod would do it because he knew I always acted in his best interest.

Marsh responded with forty-four goals in the season when we won the League Cup and were promoted to the Second Division. Many times, as in the game against Bournemouth after our Wembley triumph, I asked the referee to keep the game going longer. I was half joking, but Marsh was what the public wanted. They loved it when he controlled free kicks on his chest and blasted in goals on the volley. They loved it and wanted more.

I often thought that this was surely the start of a glittering career for the kind of player England needed. And I'm sure had Rodney Marsh gone to the right club after leaving Queen's Park Rangers he would have played for his country for a generation. He certainly should have done. He should have won at least sixty caps instead of nine.

I had left Queen's Park Rangers when they eventually let Marsh go and it was one of my biggest regrets not being around to help him choose the right club. If I had been manager and it was inevitable that Marsh was to be sold I would have persuaded, no begged, Bill Nicholson to take him to Spurs.

I kept reading that Tottenham were interested and couldn't understand why they didn't take him to White Hart Lane. He was a London player and loved the capital stage; it has always puzzled me why Spurs didn't buy Rodney Marsh.

The day he decided to join Manchester City and partner up with their colourful and controversial team manager Malcolm Allison I was at home in Epsom. I heard the news on the radio and didn't really expect to see Rod. But, to his credit, he popped around.

I remember the occasion well because I was scrubbing my front doorstep and caught sight of his little sports car as I was kneeling down with my brush and bucket. Rodney was full of talk of money and contracts and I thought then how he had changed. I felt like knocking his head off, all the common sense we had drummed into him seemed to have been forgotten. 'Think about football and your future as well,' I told him.

I don't know whether he did forget, but at the end of the day, at the end of his career, I'm sure that Rodney Marsh is disappointed with himself. I bet he says to himself 'Why didn't I do those things?' He would never admit it publicly but I am willing to bet that Rodney has big regrets. Deep down he knows he should have done better. He should have won more.

When he was playing for England I used to sit in my armchair and cry. I felt like climbing through the television screen and getting out there with him, just the way we did in training at Queen's Park Rangers. I wanted to shout and encourage him, he seemed to be letting the game – and perhaps life too – pass him by.

England never saw the real Rodney Marsh, and I don't know if football did after he went to Manchester City. It was the wrong club for him. When they didn't do it, they had someone to blame – and they certainly blamed Marshy.

All Rodney Marsh ever wanted to do was play football.

Then somewhere along the line he lost himself in our game, somewhere, somehow he found he couldn't cope with English football. Someone has got to take the blame, someone who was in charge of him. I don't think Allison was the right man for Rodney and life suddenly became complicated and complex for a boy who had always made everything look simple.

He certainly wasn't the same person when I signed Rodney and George Best for Fulham in August 1976. I signed them to give us a boost and, for a while, it worked. But I remember telling a girl reporter who came down to interview Marsh, Best and Bobby Moore for her paper: 'Luv, you don't bully superstars like other players, you try and understand them.' And, from a distance, I never really understood Rodney Marsh after he and I went our separate ways.

Malcolm Macdonald was different from Marsh. He didn't need telling he was going places. Malcolm knew what he wanted; he wanted to be the best and play for the best. And once he got that in his sights nothing and no one was going to blow him off course. He was good at making people stand up and take notice. Even in his early days at Luton Town if anyone stuck a microphone underneath Malcolm's nose he would say the right things without even trying. This was one of his great strengths.

On the pitch he could score great goals and off it he was an ambassador. It made people aware of him all the time; the press, of course, loved him, and he soon had a reputation as a player who was going places.

Macdonald was a joy to manage after we had converted him from a full back to a centre forward. He loved scoring goals and wanted more action all the time. He was hungry to show the world that at Kenilworth Road football had found someone who might just score goals for England better than anyone since Jimmy Greaves.

I first laid eyes on Macdonald on a Saturday afternoon playing for Fulham reserves at Luton. Harry Haslam and I had hurried back from our match at Tranmere the previous night because, once again, Fulham's retained list included some interesting names; once again, I thought, they were throwing experience away for nothing.

The first thing that struck me about Macdonald, apart from his strength, was his speed. He was playing at left back and could give his winger five yards and still catch him up with ease. In the programme I read that in October he had been Fulham's leading scorer in the first team and I couldn't understand why he had been returned to left back. It is a position that is one of the hardest to adjust to but if Macdonald was good at scoring why wasn't he still used up front?

We decided to make an offer and, typically in football, as soon as a club starts taking an interest in a player the selling manager becomes worried. I offered £4,000 and you could hear Fulham thinking 'That Alec Stock is a clever old boy, this Macdonald must be worth more than that.'

The fee went up to £18,000 by the time we arranged to travel to Fulham again for talks with the player. I remember that day so well because just outside Wembley our car broke down and Harry Haslam had to mend a puncture. I am absolutely no good at mending things and, anyway, Harry has got such big hands he didn't even need a jack! He was covered in grease and grime by the time we arrived late for our appointment but it was worth it.

Macdonald is not a particularly tall man and yet it is his physique that strikes you. He is as wide as a house. He had been waiting hours for us to arrive and clearly didn't have a clue what was going on when we began our interview. 'Fill me in' I asked him as Harry got cleaned up. 'Why don't they like you here, what's the problem?'

Malcolm had clearly become disillusioned with football and he explained that Fulham didn't think he could play and that the great Johnny Haynes was making life difficult for him.

He seemed an honest open boy so we signed him. He was earning £25 a week at Craven Cottage and £10 of that went on a small flat he lived in with his wife and daughter. We gave him £35 a week and spent another £200 on a little cottage that backed onto Luton's ground and gave him the key.

From that day he thought the sun shone out of Luton and we were pleased to have him. If you believe in players you have got to give them a little and I like to think this was another example of how I have tried to treat players over the years. We treated Macdonald fairly and he responded with goals that almost took us into the First Division.

His first game for us, however, was at outside left although it didn't take Harry, coach Jimmy Andrews, and I long to realize that his strength was up front. We made him a better player and Malcolm was very willing to learn.

Jimmy Andrews deserves a lot of credit for Macdonald's progress in football, certainly more credit than me. He spent days working with Malcolm, teaching him the art of goal-scoring and Malcolm was good, very good. One of his finest assets was the way he could shrug off mistakes. He was never afraid to miss.

At Queen's Park Rangers we had had Marsh and Allen and now it was Macdonald and Don Givens, another player we picked up for peanuts from Manchester United. They hit it off immediately and if it hadn't been for the Vehicle and General crash I'm sure Luton would have gone all the way through and probably won something big.

It was impossible to keep the side together however after we reluctantly sold Macdonald to Newcastle. If you start to sell at a 'small club' others want to follow. They want a taste of the big time too, and overnight you lose something you have worked so hard to build up; it breaks your heart.

If Harry, Jimmy and I had been a partnership in any other business we would have been thanked for our achievements and sent off to the South of France as a reward. In football they strip you of your assets and say 'Go on, do it again.' And if you don't they start to whisper that you are slipping. They start to say that Alec Stock isn't quite as good as we first thought.

Malcolm responded superbly right to the last minute.

Newcastle had offered £150,000 and we knew they were in the crowd again to take probably a final look at their new centre forward. I told Malcolm the situation before the kick-off and said 'Son, if you want to make a few bob out of life, today is the time to do it. Newcastle are in the stand and they want to see you score. So do I.'

Macdonald got three that day and not only did it secure his transfer but I managed to squeeze another £30,000 out of Newcastle. His price went up £10,000 a goal overnight! I thought that was lovely, a good old bit of business.

'SuperMac' as he is affectionately known now wherever he goes, scored some wonderful goals for us at Luton. Goals that football wanted to see, big spectacular shots that made people stand up and ask 'Who the hell is that?' I remember a hat-trick against Nottingham Forest in the FA Cup when we lost at home 3-4 and another treble in a televised match away to Sheffield Wednesday.

Those goals at Hillsborough made you purr and I think it was the performance that probably persuaded Newcastle to buy. Television can influence an awful lot of people and Newcastle had obviously been impressed with what they had seen. For it wasn't long before former manager Joe Harvey and director, the late Stan Seymour, were on the phone.

I felt sorry for Sheffield Wednesday because they had decided to use our visit as an occasion to invite all their old internationals back to Hillsborough. They were all there sitting in the stand, and the man who controlled the electric scoreboard decided to introduce them to the crowd just as Macdonald got our third.

'We would like to welcome today' the lights flashed and before the list was finished the crowd invited them all onto the pitch to play. 'Come on lads, they can do better than our lot today' the shout went up. 'Come on Wednesday, send them all on as substitutes!'

Newcastle in the end proved good for Macdonald. They turned him into an idol and he went from strength to strength, using his goals to woo them and his gift of the gab to win over the Newcastle public. At the time of his transfer, however, I was praying that a big London club would come in. Like Rodney Marsh, I felt that Macdonald belonged to the South and that it would be a better platform for him.

Dave Sexton, then at Chelsea, contacted me a few days after the deal had gone through and said: 'Alec, why did you sell to Newcastle, we would have bought him!' I still can't understand why Dave didn't move earlier, why he, like so many other managers in transfer deals, waited for a positive move from someone else before reacting.

Macdonald, however, probably feels happier than Rodney Marsh today in his contribution to football. They both no doubt have regrets. All I know is that I was very lucky to have them and sign them; we helped each other a little along the way.

8 A Little Thing called Pride

Football management is all about a little thing called pride. A pride that comes with achievement, winning, being able to say 'I did that; that is my team out there and we have worked damn hard together.'

Getting to Wembley for a Cup Final is when your pride really blows up inside you and bursts. The moment you realize that the time has come to walk down the tunnel and out into the daylight, out into the spotlight. It's a feeling of elation, complete satisfaction. It is a time to think of family and friends, time to wave at your wife and know that she is just as proud, a time when a million things flash through your mind and disappear just as quickly as you try and take in everything.

Behind you there are eleven men who are just as proud, a team who want to enjoy themselves as much as you. It is a little private family walking out together, a group of people who are thinking only of themselves at that moment but know that for ninety minutes they must work like hell together. You like to win, of course, but, quite frankly, being there is what matters.

I have made that walk twice and although that doesn't sound a lot in thirty-five years I am one of the lucky ones. I have been there and I'm delighted that I managed to take players like Tony Hazell, Frank Sibley, Keith Sanderson, Mark Lazarus, Peter Mellor, Alan Slough, John Mitchell and Viv Busby – players who perhaps didn't dream of playing at Wembley – to a Cup Final.

I have also experienced the wonderful feeling of winning when in 1967 Queen's Park Rangers came from 0-2 down to beat West Bromwich Albion 3-2 in the League Cup Final and the bitter disappointment of playing badly when Fulham lost 0-2 to West Ham in the 1975 Cup Final.

They are memories that no one can ever take away from me and I have a photograph from each of those years hanging proudly in my new home in Bournemouth to remind me. I have never been a great collector of mementoes, my daughters have most of my awards and cuttings, but those two photographs do mean a lot.

Many times over the years I have thought about my two Finals and in the repeated analysis I have come to the conclusion that after the many hours of planning, build-up and waiting, it was two three-minute talk-ins I had with my players that made the difference between winning and losing.

Mine was the story of the snatched conversation you have with your team at half-time, the few minutes when you know you must say the right things. I obviously got it right with Rangers and wrong with Fulham.

There is one thing at Wembley I will never understand and that is the seating arrangements for the two managers and their staff. There is no dug-out to sit in and, to make matters worse, the benches are so close together you are sitting completely on top of each other.

There is no point in screaming and shouting or trying to encourage your team because you are so far away from the players. I have always had a close rapport with my skipper but at Wembley that connection is severed. A manager has just to sit in silence.

You are completely divorced from the play and there is absolutely no chance of passing on little messages or making tactical switches because your opponent can hear every word and watch every movement you make. You can't even suffer or celebrate in private. On both occasions I felt like going for a stroll and getting the hell out of it.

It was a relief when the half-time whistle went in 1967.

We were 0-2 down and struggling but at least I suddenly felt involved again. I knew that it was up to me to lift a few heads and try and change things. As I walked briskly around the dog track towards the dressing-rooms (I wanted to run but felt it would have been a sign of panic) I thought to myself: 'You have got about two minutes to sort this little lot out. All our supporters are asking themselves what has gone wrong and you have got to make sure you say the right things.'

At 0-2 of course it was fairly easy. We were not playing well and I just laid into the team: 'This is the greatest day in your lives and you are responding like that. If we are going to lose let's lose with a bit of pride. Do you all want to look back on this day and have nightmares?'

Then I turned on our two front men Les Allen and Rodney Marsh who hadn't done a thing in the first half. 'You two can take your fingers out or stay in the dressing-room.' You are talking all the time to players who are scurrying around doing their own thing; some of the Rangers players changed studs, others were in the toilet, two or three washed and others just sat back reflecting on the disastrous first half. But it worked. No one will ever know really why it changed, but the players responded.

The Fulham talk-in was different. Again we were the underdogs and most people expected us to lose, but at half-time it was 0-0 and although it was a drab old game and we were not playing particularly well, it was a good result at that time.

I should probably have had a go at them and told them that more effort was needed, and demanded more from certain players. I didn't and made the mistake of allowing the half-time break to drift by 'Well done lads, it's not going too badly. Keep it going, jolly, jolly'. It was the wrong approach and I should have used some good old industrial language. But I didn't, and we lost. It is easy, I know, to look back and reminisce and yet my half-time talk to the Fulham players goes down as another little regret in my life.

There is never any real thought of getting to Wembley

when you set out at the start of every season. There is hope of success of course, and that hope was directed at promotion when Third Division Queen's Park Rangers began the 1966-67 season.

The League Cup was just a little bonus and not even a 5-0 win in the first round against Colchester and a nap hand for Alan Wilks stirred the side up. Our thoughts were definitely on the Second Division, especially when we drew 1-1 at Aldershot in the second round and had to postpone a league match the following week because of the replay.

On the way home from Aldershot Jim Gregory said to me 'Promotion is everything, I had rather you lost tonight, we can't afford replays.' He was right and we began to curse the League Cup although we beat Aldershot 2-0 in the replay to earn an away draw at Swansea in the next round. We beat them too and suddenly we had arrived in the fourth round with a home draw against powerful Leicester City.

We may have been Third Division and going for promotion but we feared no one at home and turned it on against Leicester, beating them 4-2. Carlisle were next, again at home, and we accounted for them too by two goals to one.

The players were now getting excited about Wembley and a little bit of football history. The draw gave us First Division Birmingham in a two-leg semi final and I thought our cup run was over when Barry Bridges, the former Chelsea star, scored for Birmingham in the first minutes up at St Andrews. I would have settled for a 1-0 defeat and a damn good second leg at the Bush although I hadn't anticipated going behind so early in the game.

Like so many times in that season we responded superbly and produced a wonderful second half performance to trounce them 4-1. We hit a peak that night and I'm sure that if the game had gone on another six minutes it would have been ten.

The second leg was a formality and we won 3-1. It didn't stop dear old Laurie Pignon, then football correspondent of the old *Daily Sketch* and now the *Daily Mail's* chief tennis writer, saying afterwards, 'Bit of a drab game, Alec.' 'Laurie'

I replied, 'How can it be a drab game when we have just beaten a First Division side 7-2 on aggregate and got to Wembley. You should be painting us as one of the great achievements of the sixties.'

West Brom had beaten West Ham 6-2 in the other semi final and so on 4 March 1967, Queen's Park Rangers walked out at Wembley and the team picked itself: Peter Springett; Tony Hazell, Jim Langley; Frank Sibley, Ron Hunt, Mike Keen; Mark Lazarus, Keith Sanderson, Les Allen, Rodney Marsh, Roger Morgan. Roger's twin brother Ian was the substitute.

We froze in the first half and little Clive Clark, who six years before had been QPR's feed man for the then top scorer Brian Bedford, tore us apart. He gave Hazell the run around and scored both of West Brom's goals. Clive had been sold to West Brom primarily because it was a good price and also because he had been getting kicked to death by Third Division defenders. It was a sale that at the time probably cost us promotion.

In the second half Roger Morgan soon scored and all of us sitting on the bench, including old friend and journalist Reg Hayter, began to sense a revival. I don't know why or how the players responded the way they did; I can still see Rodney scoring his marvellous equalizer and Lazarus, bless him, tucking away the winner.

I think Reg still carries the bruises from the buffeting I gave him in my excitement. It was a marvellous feeling and I didn't run this time on the way back to the dressing-rooms. I strolled round the ground savouring every moment. It was almost as if we had been meant to win that day.

I am a great believer in fate and in history repeating itself and it's interesting now to look back and recall how in 1967 Queen's Park Rangers beat Carlisle in the quarter final and Birmingham in the semis, and eight years later Fulham did exactly the same. Was there a sign on Fulham and Alec Stock that year because Second Division Fulham won every game away from home to get to Wembley?

The long, long road began against Hull in the third round.

We drew 1-1 at Craven Cottage in front of nearly nine thousand people and Wembley seemed a million miles away. Viv Busby's two goals in the replay gave us a 2-2 draw after extra time and after 210 minutes we were still in the cup but not over the first hurdle. When you are the Fulhams of this world it is money the cup gives you; that is your priority when you set out. A couple of good results and a home draw against one of the big boys.

We had to go to Leicester and a neutral ground to finish with Hull and Alan Slough finally broke the deadlock with the only goal of the game. If we thought Hull had been a tough nut to crack, Brian Clough's Nottingham Forest was waiting. We drew 0-0 at home, 1-1 away after extra time, 1-1 in the second replay, again after extra time, before Busby scored twice again in the cup to shake off Forest in a third replay.

Now, surely, the luck of the draw would give us a home draw and the chance to make a few bob for the club. It gave us a giant all right but we had to travel again, this time to First Division Everton. We had no chance on paper and the critics, quite rightly, wrote us off.

I suppose this next story will only really appeal to Liverpool supporters although it does prove just how much rivalry there is on Merseyside between Liverpool and Everton. We had travelled up to Everton on the Friday night and, while the players rested on match day morning, Bill Taylor, my coach, and I were at a bit of a loose end. So we decided to jump into a taxi, take the skips down to Goodison Park and have a wander around the ground to taste the atmosphere and kill a couple of hours.

The taxi driver soon realized who we were and made it perfectly clear that he was a very committed Liverpool fan. 'I'll be praying for you this afternoon, Mr Stock. Do you think you can beat them? Please God, beat them.' The taxi dropped us outside the main entrance and Bill and I began to struggle with the skips. They are heavy and awkward to lift and we clearly needed a hand to get them into the dressing-rooms. But before I could ask our taxi driver for help he shook his head defiantly and said: 'I'm sorry Mr Stock, but I wouldn't cross that threshold if you gave me £50.'

We had our finest hour against Everton, the best performance and result of our cup run and one of the outstanding displays while I was at Fulham. Again Viv Busby did the trick with his third cup double although it was a magnificent team performance. Bobby Moore at the back brought out the best in the young full back Les Strong, Mullery ran his legs off in midfield as he shouted and encouraged the young players around him and up front Busby made a bit of a name for himself.

The dressing-room, as you can appreciate, was a marvellous place to be. There was drinking, dancing; the players knew how well they had played and were enjoying their big moment. I certainly hadn't expected to win this game and told Bill Bothwell, the former Tranmere chairman and BBC radio commentator who died in 1980, of my surprise and delight, when he interviewed me for *Sports Report* at the back of the Goodison Park main stand after the match.

In my excitement I had forgotten all about the cup draw for the quarter finals that was being made at 5 o'clock and Bill persuaded me to stay on and listen to it live. I have always thought that it was a bad thing to make the draw directly after cup matches and my fears were proved when we were drawn away to Carlisle. I made up my mind there and then not to tell the players who our next opponents were. They still had their heads in the clouds and the last thing they wanted to know was that we were on our way to Carlisle. So I let the party roll all the way back to London.

The match at Carlisle was one of the worst games I have sat through in my life. It was dreadful, boring stuff that made you want to crawl up and ask the Football Association if we could start all over again. Our goalkeeper, Peter Mellor, kept us in the match with some superb acrobatic saves before Carlisle made a hash of a back pass and Les Barrett nipped in for our winning goal. It was the kind of match that just had to be settled on a mistake.

The best part of the day was the party on the way home,

Above: Alan Mullery – 'a great captain' – and I talk tactics at Fulham. (*Photo:* News Group Newspapers)

Below: My two greatest fans, daughters Elizabeth (left) and Sarah (right). (*Photo: Daily Express)*

My first day at Arsenal. 'Let's see how fit you are, hmmm?' (*Photo:* Keystone)

Above: The late Gigi Peronace welcomes me to Roma. (*Photo: Daily Mail)*
Below: George Best and Rodney Marsh – welcome to Fulham. (*Photo:* Keystone)

Above: This really is the White City – 'Can we play, ref?' (*Photo: Acton Gazette*)

Below: A very proud day for me as I receive the freedom of the Borough of Hammersmith.

The dugout is a manager's castle for ninety minutes. Here (from left to right) physio Ron Woolnough, myself, coach John Collins and my right-hand man Bill Taylor watch and worry during Fulham's FA Cup semi final with Birmingham.

Queen's Park Rangers chairman, Jim Gregory, shows the League Cup to former Football League president, Len Shipman.

Manager of the Month – 'It's not a bad old life.'

The glory of Wembley ... Mark Lazarus turns away after scoring Queen's Park Rangers' dramatic winner in the League Cup Final. Roger Morgan (No.11), Mike Keen (No. 6) and Rodney Marsh celebrate.

... and the disappointment. I console John Mitchell after West Ham have beaten Fulham in the 1975 FA Cup Final. Goalkeeper Peter Mellor is on the left.

The old master. Bobby Moore and myself at Fulham's training ground. (*Photo:* The Press Association)

The pressure is always the same. Bournemouth players get the message. (*Photo: Sun)*

although a massive traffic jam in Carlisle almost made us miss our train. We had booked the restaurant car on the express inter-city train back to London and the players were already planning how many bottles of lager they could drink when we ran straight into a traffic jam a few miles from the station. It was left to Bobby Moore to hang out of the coach and direct the cars and people out of the way. I'm sure the Carlisle public had never seen anything like it before, England's former World Cup captain dangling from a coach and asking people to move.

Our semi final against Birmingham was played at Hillsborough. John Mitchell, in the side for the injured Jim Conway, scored the kind of goal that centre forwards dream about, a dipping volley from outside the area that flew into the top corner. We should have won that day and Birmingham's equalizer, a scrappy goal from their centre half Joe Gallagher, made it all the more frustrating.

And so to Maine Road for the replay, our eleventh match in the competition. How much more had the players left to give, was there another fairytale left? Like Queen's Park Rangers all those years ago, were we meant to win this semi final? Yes we were.

I can still see John Mitchell bursting through and scoring our winning goal off his stomach in the last seconds of extra time. Kisses, cuddles, even the sight of Bobby Moore, the man who never showed emotion, running the length of the pitch to jump on the bundle of players, that was our celebration. It was certainly a moment to treasure.

And as the referee's whistle blew to put us into the final, everything and everybody around me went berserk. Ron Woolnough's bucket was emptied over someone, Bill Taylor and I did a little dance on the touchline and out in the middle someone tried to stop our skipper, Alan Mullery, joining in the celebration. Mullery turned round to register his protest only to find Alex Stepney, the Manchester United goalkeeper and an old friend, smiling at him. Alex had been so pleased for Mullery that he had charged out of his seat to join in the pitch party.

Fulham had never seen anything quite like those weeks building up to the cockney cup final against West Ham. The houses around Craven Cottage were decorated in black and white – we even took the team on a walkabout – and hundreds of old friends turned up daily to say 'Hello', 'Well done', and 'Have you got a ticket to spare?'

I was duty bound, of course, to get the two 'old men' Alan Mullery and Moore unscathed to Wembley, particularly Moore against his old club. I had the audacity to ask them if they would prefer not to play in our last Second Division match of the season, away to Bristol City, seven days before the final.

You would have thought I had asked them not to play at Wembley. They are two very proud professionals and they only don't play when they are injured. Anyway, I was put firmly in my place and nothing more was said although I kept my fingers crossed all the way through the Bristol City match because Wembley that year without Moore or Mullery would not have been the same.

The other Fulham players had not experienced anything like the build-up before. There were cameras, spotlights and interviews every day and even the scare of reading the small print on their contracts to see what it said about reaching Wembley.

The Fulham players had not dreamt about playing in the FA Cup Final when their contracts were drawn up at the beginning of the season and Peter Mellor, the players' union representative, was faced with a number of very worried players. 'What are we going to do Pete?' they asked him. 'We never thought about appearance money and bonuses for Wembley. Is that in the contract? Are we going to get anything?'

Bobby Moore only rubbed salt in the wound when he said to Mellor: 'You should have sorted that out, old son, shouldn't leave anything like that off a contract.' It was only a tease, of course, and everything was sorted out in the end. The Fulham players got their reward for taking the club to Wembley for the only time in its history. And quite rightly so.

The final was a big disappointment. We suffered a blow in the week before the game when our young full back Les Strong was ruled out with an ankle injury. It was a terrible shame for the lad for he had done so well and improved so much alongside Bob Moore that people were even talking about an England cap.

I had to play a youngster called John Fraser and was also not completely happy about the match fitness of Jim Conway and Alan Slough. These are not excuses, only thoughts after the event. We couldn't have any excuse the way we played and in the end took our satisfaction from taking part.

I also have regrets when I look back at not giving the substitute's shirt to John Dowie, a young Scot who had done so well for us in previous years. I plumped instead for the experience of Barry Lloyd and had to tell a broken-hearted Dowie that he was not in the twelve. Another little regret.

The atmosphere and pressure of the occasion certainly got to me and I needed an injection before the start to help calm me down. I'm pleased I had it because I was soon pushing my hands through my hair in frustration as both sides struggled to give the crowd what they wanted, a spectacle.

We only looked like scoring twice, a header from John Lacy in the first half and a point blank volley from John Mitchell that hit West Ham goalkeeper Mervyn Day and rebounded to safety, midway through the second half.

The rest of the game was scrappy and not the 'great game' we had all dreamed about. West Ham began to expose our right full back John Cutbush and Alan Taylor, West Ham's new striker who had scored twice against Arsenal and Ipswich in previous rounds, kept up his record with another double.

The dressing-room afterwards of course was nothing like 1967. It smelt of anticlimax and disappointment and there is not much you can say in these circumstances. The players were left to their thoughts and allowed to unwind at the after-match banquet. Moore and Mullery didn't seem too disappointed. They had, after all, seen it all before. The fact that they had been back to Wembley in the twilight of their careers was enough to celebrate later that night.

Losers' banquets are usually events to avoid although I like to think that Fulham's was a happy occasion. The club were so delighted at getting to Wembley that they soon forgot the score and what had happened a few hours earlier. And when the groundsman ordered a bottle of champagne at four in the morning I knew it hadn't been a bad old night!

Being a loser at Wembley leaves you with only one thing, your memories and your regrets. I was therefore very happy and honoured to receive a tribute from the Borough of Hammersmith. They wanted to recognize my achievements at taking two of their teams, Queen's Park Rangers and Fulham, to Wembley and I was made an honorary Freeman of the London Borough of Hammersmith.

A little bit of nonsense, you might say, but it is an honour given for exceptional services to the community and it means that I will go down in history as achieving something. As I said, football management is all about a little thing called pride.

9 Strangers in the Night

Bobby Moore. There is very little I can add in tribute to a player who is admired throughout the world. Apart from being one of the greatest players this country has produced, Moore has what every professional dreams about, the respect of all players and managers.

I was delighted when Moore agreed to join Fulham from West Ham and very proud to have him at my club. He is a gentleman on and off the field. Moore always trained and played to the best of his ability for me and then went about his business. He was an ambassador for the club. The one thing you knew when you signed Bobby Moore was that life with him would be very pleasant.

It is therefore with sadness and a great deal of bitterness that I am forced to use the great man as the central figure of this chapter on referees. It is impossible to ignore because what happened at Burnden Park, Bolton on Tuesday, 5 October 1976, represents the most controversial referee incident I have been involved with. It also emphasizes the massive gap between players and managers and referees.

Bobby Moore was sent off. That in itself proves that some very strange things went on at Bolton in our League Cup Third Round replay. The referee was Kevin McNally, who has since parted company with the Football League and been taken off the list. Mr McNally will always go down in history as the man who sent off Bobby Moore. I don't know whether he is proud of that; certainly no one that night was proud of his handling of the game.

I never thought the day would come when I was forced to lead my team off the pitch or I would see players crying in frustration and saying they wanted to 'give Bolton the game!' And directors agreeing with them.

McNally forced all that and I will never forgive him for it. Yet he was never alone and there are referees around today of whom players are very wary. It can't be good for the sport when a manager has to say just before the kick-off 'Now don't forget who is in charge today fellas, be careful. Keep one eye on the referee. You know what he is like.' The players go out knowing that they are not going to be allowed to really enjoy themselves.

At Bolton there was no hint of controversy throughout the match. I had sent out a very young team, with a couple of old stagers to hold things together, and they had responded superbly. I was delighted with them and at ten past nine we had won 2-1 with goals from John Mitchell and Ernie Howe ... or so I thought.

No anxiety, frustration or anger had built up inside me during the match. I just sat in my grandstand seat and thought 'Well played fellas, lovely little victory. We might just have a few gin and tonics on the way home'.

Slowly I began to smell a rat, and five minutes later I hurried down to the dug-out and asked the linesman 'What's going on?'. 'Don't blame me, Mr Stock' he said 'I have been signalling for five minutes.' 'I'm not blaming you' I snorted back at him. 'I just want to know what is going on.' The players, especially the younger ones, had begun to become angry and mystified, moving over to the touchline to ask why the game was going on for so long.

As the minutes ticked by I knew we were in for one of those nights. The atmosphere had changed and it got worse by the second. In the middle of it all was Mr McNally, the one man with the power and the only man who knew the answers.

There is one main thing players and managers ask for

from a referee and that is to be fair. To me the man in the middle has always been the custodian of fair play. Nothing else. Everyone is allowed to make mistakes and referees are no exception. Heaven forbid, players do stupid things during a game and managers are always full of regrets. They watch and think 'Should have played so and so today.'

The other quality you pray a referee has is consistency. You hope he doesn't box anything where it matters. 'Please make your mistakes in the middle of the park where it doesn't matter' you say as the game begins. And when a goal is scored please be 'spot on.' Have no hesitation, no doubts. When the ball hits the back of the net and the crowd goes up in celebration say 'yes, that was a goal'. And make sure it was.

Too often in recent seasons there have been games of great doubt, decisions which puzzle and incidents that are discussed for days and torn apart on television and in the newspapers. It is not good for the image of the game. At Bolton all my fears arrived in one sickening explosion. All that is wrong in refereeing happened that night. So many things went on in a short time. I still can't understand how they were allowed to happen.

By the time we had played five minutes over time the crowd began to get restless, they couldn't understand what was happening. John Evanson jogged over to take a corner and the crowd began to abuse him and throw things. McNally seemed to be blaming Evanson for 'time wasting'. The crowd immediately switched their aggravation to him and there followed a few seconds of anger that only added fire to the situation.

We had played nine minutes over time by my watch and it was almost twenty past nine when our goalkeeper Peter Mellor punched out a cross from the right and the Bolton left back hammered it back into the top corner. The equalizer. Pandemonium! The Bolton crowd flooded onto the pitch in a mixture of relief, confusion and delight. At that moment I'm sure no one at Burnden Park knew what was going on.

I was completely flabbergasted and began to think I was dreaming when someone raced up to tell me 'Moore has been sent off'. That is the last thing you think is going to happen, even on a night when nothing is surprising anymore. Apparently, he had said something to the referee, words probably that most of the Fulham party would have liked to aim at McNally at that moment.

Young players were now crying. They all looked to me for guidance and Terry Bullivant, the midfield kid Fulham later sold to Aston Villa for £250,000, summed up the players' feelings completely: 'Boss, can't we give them the game, I don't want to play in that match anymore.'

I had to make a decision and for the first and only time in my career I led a team off the pitch. Some order had to be restored and I took the players back into the dressing-room. It was an instant decision but one, in similar circumstances, I would do again. I still believe I was right.

Our dressing-room was just like the pitch, people tearing around in bewilderment. It was chaos and Sir Eric Miller met me at the door with this bombshell 'Alec, let's give them the game.' And the frightening thing was that most of the players agreed with him. 'You can't do that' I screamed back at the team and told the directors to get out. The players and I needed a few seconds to think. After all, the ball was suddenly completely in our court.

Experienced men like Moore, John Lacy and Mellor, players with coaching badges and numerous qualifications, didn't know what to do for the best. No one was in the mood to go out again and play extra time. Suddenly we were brought back to reality by a loud knock on the door. McNally stood in the doorway flanked by two big policemen. 'I want you on the pitch in one minute otherwise you forfeit the game' he demanded.

My experienced players immediately turned on him. 'That's another rule you don't know' they shouted. 'You can't forfeit games.' But we went out, and we drew. We held on. When the dust had settled the inquests started and there was a lot of talking to do.

No matter how you bring players up they can't help reacting to situations like that. They think to themselves 'referees make vital mistakes' and the gap between us and them is pushed even wider apart. It is unfortunate but players begin to lump all referees together.

All my players at Bolton were confused. They thought that McNally had pushed them too far; they were provoked and got to the point where they reacted. And in the end, it is always the clubs who are wrong. The referee, in the authorities' eyes, must be right.

The most honest man for me at Burnden Park was a chap called Freddie Pye, the chairman of Stockport County who had been a guest of Bolton manager Ian Greaves. A few days later he sent me a copy of a letter he had posted to the Football Association and the Football League. In it he said: 'I am a friend of Ian Greaves and was invited by Bolton to the game and so, obviously, wanted them to win. But if the things that happened that night had happened to my club I would have withdrawn from the League.'

The result of it all was that I was called before the top brass at the Football Association's Lancaster Gate headquarters in London. I had been charged with bringing the game into disrepute for leading my team off the field of play. I think it must have been the only time that the top brass – former leaders, Football Association chairman Sir Harold Thompson, disciplinary chairman Vernon Stokes, and League president Lord Westwood – had sat together on one committee. I told them straight 'Gentlemen, I am here to tell you one thing, I think he was wrong.' Well, they threw my case out and, I believe, justice was done. McNally has now left the League list and that decision, I hope, was not directly linked to our match at Bolton. But those are the facts.

On another occasion I appeared before a disciplinary committee after a difference of opinion with a referee who had reported me for ungentlemanly conduct. The panel refused to accept that I was deaf and after a furious row I threatened to send them my pension book for proof. I was really annoyed. The lack of manners in high places is often quite frightening.

I was fined £60 that time, only for the referee to be crossed off the League list the following season. I took it as a back-handed compliment and felt like writing to the men who sat on that committee and queried my judgment and asking for my money back. As I have said, people who run the game should listen more to the professionals.

I am a great believer in incidents and wrong decisions levelling themselves out in football and, quite frankly, I have not complained very much over the years about the standard of refereeing. Lately, however, I have been very worried. Is the standard falling?

Clubs no longer give referees marks for performance and I believe that is a great shame. The League clearly thought the marks and comments by clubs were always related to the result but certainly in my case the referees' marks were given for exactly what we saw.

Most clubs now miss saying to the referee 'Well played, you had a damn good game.' It was always nice to see a fella win something and it was players and managers enjoying a little contact with referees. Now the referee is marked by an assessor who sits in the stand and no way is that a better system.

The Moore sending off, apart from surprising the rest of football, also completed a week that badly damaged my unofficial disciplinary record. I have always been proud that only a handful of my players have been sent off but in the space of four days George Best was dismissed at Southampton and Moore ordered off at Bolton.

There had been so few before that little burst of unexpected activity that my memory clouds when I try and think of the names. I remember Alan Slough at Luton and Orient's Tom Johnstone but after that I don't recall. I still believe there have been only about five and that, in thirty-five years, must be one of the best records in football.

There are still a few referees around today who worry players. Referees who scare players. You are almost expecting controversy, anticipating that there will be wrong decisions made. A question I have always asked myself is where and when do referees bring the game into disrepute?

If a manager does a bad job, or the board of directors feel they want a change, he is sacked. Players get dropped or hauled before a disciplinary committee for misconduct on the field of play. Why is there no such code of conduct for referees?

There is surely a case for examining a referee's record. Is he a good referee if he takes more names than anyone else; is that what they believe keeping control is all about? Certain referees maintain discipline by slamming players, arguing on the pitch and getting too involved. They seem to want to be noticed. If I was a referee who took names at the rate of one or two a match I would feel damned inefficient. I would start to question my ability.

At Bournemouth in the Fourth Division the referee, I'm sure, is the best-paid person who walks out on to Dean Court on match days. His fee for being a referee and travelling expenses make him the top earner of the day and, in return, we should be allowed to expect a top class performance. It doesn't often work out like that. If our man has been around in the First Division that season he arrives at Bournemouth on an ego trip. He has come down to teach us a lesson.

Referees however should be careful. They are demonstrating to the public what they are like as men. And the public are not fools, they represent the best assessors of all. There is no hiding place out in the middle, the public soon find out if you are good enough.

But the public do want to respect the referee. They don't really want to shout and moan at the man in black because he is the last person they have come to see. They want him to have personality and a bit of character. But most of all they want him to have quiet authority that goes unnoticed until at the end of the game you realize that the match had no trouble at all and ran smoothly from start to finish. The fans want to say when they are analysing the game, 'Didn't old so-and-so have a good game. Never saw or heard him. Brilliant.'

Referees like Jim Finney, Gordon Hill and Jack Taylor were the kind of outstanding referees I am talking about because they had the lovely little thing called reputation. Everyone knew when they saw their names in the programme that it was going to be a good, fair game. You didn't even have to mention the referee in your pre-match talk.

Even someone like Roger Kirkpatrick, with his bald head and high running action, gave the game that little extra something. He was a character, and the crowd responded. I recall one game at Queen's Park Rangers when my daughters and a few of their friends came giggling into the guests room after the match. 'What have you lot been up to?' I said. 'Oh Dad, it's been a smashing game, we have been calling the referee baldie!' But Roger didn't mind, he knew that it was all part of his attraction.

Today the game even looks a bit grim through the eyes of a referee. It's always a matter of life and death when he talks to players. There are no laughs any more. The assessor watching his every move up in the stand has frightened him to death.

We must get referees and players closer together, we must get them to respect one another more. In Italy they employed a good system that seemed to draw our respect in both parties and for a time we used it in this country, although not with the same good results.

Before every match in Italy the referee knocked on the door and entered the dressing-room with his two linesmen. They always looked immaculate, dressed perfectly and were always big powerful men. Real smoothies. I couldn't believe it the first time it happened to me. The entire Roma side stood to attention and the skipper moved forward, shook the referee's hand, and handed him the team sheet. The referee only stayed for a couple of minutes and the air of authority was perfect. 'Gentlemen' he would say, 'I am your referee, these are my linesmen. And gentlemen, I hope you have a most excellent game.'

It was beautiful, just the right balance of authority and respect. He didn't try and show off, just quietly proved to the players who was in charge. People often criticize Continental referees and yet I always found them brilliant, no trouble at all.

When I was at Luton it was decided to allow referees into the dressing-rooms before the kick-off for the first time and you have never witnessed such a débâcle in all your life. It was a shambles and all because most referees didn't know how to handle the situation.

A fella would come in and stand in front of the players with a sheet of paper in his hand and start to read out all the things he wanted to see and all the things players couldn't do. After a few minutes both his linesmen had their heads in the air in bored embarrassment and all round the dressing-room all you could see was bare backsides and jockstraps. The players had just turned their backs, thinking 'Oh we have got another right one here.'

Then there was Jack Taylor. Good old Jack, in he would come and say: 'These are my two linesmen and fellas I hope you have a good afternoon. If I box anything I will be very sorry.' And that was it, lovely. It's all you wanted, no fuss, no mucking about and the players knew they were in for a good game of football.

The oldest and most infuriating saying some of them would use was: 'Lads I know all about the over-the-top tackle and I don't want to see it in this game.' Well, I have watched football closely for thirty-five years and can honestly say that I can only remember a few times when there has been a tackle that stank of over-the-top.

People like to talk about football being dirty, and too tough and physical. For me it isn't as hard as it used to be, and as for over-the-top I'm sure hardly anyone can remember seeing more than one or two really bad tackles. And yet some referees still want to make an issue of it before a ball has been kicked.

One golden rule I have taught myself over the years is

never argue with a referee over the condition of the pitch. If you think it's unplayable don't say so. You are not going to change his mind; I once tried to when I was at Queen's Park Rangers and indirectly it cost us promotion.

We were playing at Halifax on a day when you would have thought twice about going outside the front door. It was bitterly cold and there was snow and ice everywhere. Halifax was no exception and their pitch was rock hard and, I thought, unplayable.

At two o'clock when we got to the ground the referee was already out on the pitch. I took one look and said: 'I'm not happy to play on that.' He clearly thought the game could go ahead and ordered the gates to be unlocked and the crowd allowed in. As we were walking into the dressing-room I said 'If you start, I bet we won't finish.'

I couldn't believe how well we played in the first half. Rangers adapted to the conditions superbly and at half-time were 2-0 up. I was relieved and delighted when we walked off, only for the referee to bring me down to earth. 'You are right, Alec' he said. 'We can't finish, it's too dangerous.' And with that he abandoned the game. In the rearranged match a few weeks later we only drew and went on to miss out on promotion by one point. So from that day I have kept my mouth shut. The referee is always right as far as I'm concerned when it comes to pitch inspections!

If I could have one wish for the future concerning referees it is that monthly meetings should be arranged for players and managers to get to know them better. No manager knows anything about referees and the men in black are completely ignorant when it comes to player management. It is a crime when a manager has to knock politely on the referee's changing room door at the end of the game and ask him to explain an incident, booking or sending off he doesn't understand.

It is a situation that could only happen in football and the answer is usually a curt 'Everything will be in my report.' It only forces the two parties further apart, we are strangers in the night. We never meet. I don't understand why the men in power have never arranged such meetings. Why shouldn't the men who play to the laws meet the men who administer them?

They don't have to be formal discussions, a chat over a pint of beer would do. Only good can come out of something like that and a little thing called respect would help. You must have respect. At the moment players don't respect referees and, probably, vice versa. It is a ridiculous situation and also the main reason why the discipline record is so poor throughout the game.

The only time we meet the referee is on match days, probably an hour before the kick-off when everyone is rushing around. He is too worried and hot under the collar and we are under pressure; we just don't want to know each other.

Football is the only sport in which two of the most important people involved in the game are kept apart. In cricket, players have a couple of beers with the umpire and former players are encouraged to help in the administration of the game. I have been a player and manager for thirty-five years and yet in that time I have never been asked to discuss the game's problems with referees and certainly not encouraged to put my experience back into football. Cricket recognizes the ability of the ex-professional but at times football is more MCC than the MCC.

It is a gap we must close. There are only a handful of referees whom the players respect and that is not good for the game. I just don't understand why the gap has never been closed; it needs a simple thing called understanding and respect.

10 My Biggest Regret

On 7 February 1956, I left Leyton Orient for the first time to join Arsenal. It was the ultimate compliment as far as I was concerned. The First Division. The biggest club in football, a little bit of respect and style. Everything I wanted from the moment I came into management.

I had been supremely happy at Orient, enjoying the challenge of working on a shoestring and building something out of nothing. Now it was my turn to work with better players, the top facilities and money to play the transfer market. That was something I was looking forward to.

Arsenal offered me things I had never experienced before and they were exciting times building up to my first day at Highbury. I didn't really view it as a challenge, Arsenal had asked for me and they were the club to work with if you wanted to be recognized as the best.

The first day I walked into Highbury I was on cloud nine. I had thought about the job a lot and knew exactly what I hoped to achieve. I had always enjoyed working closely with players and Arsenal had some of the top men in the country. Stars like Jack Kelsey (one of the best professionals I worked with), Jim Holton, Derek Tapscott, Jimmy Bloomfield, Dave Bowen, Bill Dodgin and Danny Clapton. My two old friends, Vic Groves and Stan Charlton, were already at Highbury of course. I had sold them the previous November for £30,000 to enable Orient to buy a grandstand.

I would never have dreamt that fifty-three days later I

would be walking out on Arsenal and back across London to my 'home' at Orient. I quit Highbury as a very disappointed and disillusioned young man.

There are many regrets surrounding my career when I look back and Arsenal probably represents the biggest regret of all. I should have handled the entire situation much better. I certainly shouldn't have gone when I did and definitely not turned my back on the best job in football.

It is easy to turn back the pages and paint different pictures but I know that Arsenal and I could have had a long, happy relationship if I had stuck it out. The trouble was they never gave me a specific job. In fact it only took me a few days to realize there was no real job for me at all.

I should have pinned down the club's chairman, Sir Bracewell Smith, and secretary-manager, Tom Whittaker, to explain my exact role during the interview. Maybe I was too eager to join and it certainly never crossed my mind that I wouldn't be working with the players. I thought that was why Arsenal wanted me.

At Yeovil and Orient I had always been involved. I had always been busy, the 'worryguts' who responded to problems and minor crises. I was prepared to accept all that and more at Arsenal, but it was soon obvious that they didn't know what to do with me.

I suppose my role was that of a 'sort of coach'. There was never any question of my picking teams and having the final word on selection. That was very much the job of Tom Whittaker. They used to put me in the referee's changing room to get changed and then leave me on the fringe of training and tactics.

Tom would say to me 'Go and take the wife out Alec' when I was desperate to work and make my mark on Arsenal. I often gave my advice on players and opponents and suddenly realized that it was being ignored. Arsenal paid me £3,000 a year and for fifty-three days I didn't really earn it. I wanted to, but it was impossible.

In the sixth round of the FA Cup that year Arsenal were drawn at home to Birmingham, a team Orient had already lost to in the third round. I obviously knew a bit about Birmingham and was keen to pass on all the information and tips I could. For some reason the club asked someone else to produce a dossier on Birmingham. I couldn't understand that and when I eventually read it, I found it a bit of a joke. The report said that Jackie Stewart was Birmingham's danger man. 'But Tom' I said, 'He left Birmingham two years ago. The man you want to watch is Gordon Astle.' It was just another little mystery and I soon realized that Tom Whittaker was a nice man and a great servant to Arsenal.

The trouble was that most of my friends at Orient were still daily visitors to my home. It only added to the frustration and mixed feelings I began to have about leaving Brisbane Road in the first place.

Orient were going for promotion and I found myself worrying about them, selecting their teams in my head as well as the Arsenal teams. Harry Zussman, the Orient chairman whom I had worked with so well, began to hear stories of how unhappy I was and he really threw the cat among the pigeons when he contacted me one day and asked, 'Alec, why don't you come back?'

It was something I didn't really want to hear, and yet it was good to feel wanted again. Leyton Orient obviously still meant a great deal to me. I decided to stick it out, pushing behind me the temptation to return to Leyton Orient and the interesting challenge of getting them promotion to the Second Division.

Then one Saturday Arsenal were playing away to Sheffield United. To my horror and deep frustration I was told to stay behind and watch Aldershot reserves. I was told I could be of help in assessing the retained list. But I thought I was wasting my time, I still desperately wanted to get involved with the Arsenal first team.

My mood was a mixture of gloom and despondency when I set out on the Saturday morning. My heart, I suppose, was with Orient and my thoughts were with Arsenal; my teams playing at opposite ends of the country and where was I going? To watch Aldershot reserves.

To take my mind off things and to stop me just hanging about at home in the morning I left early to take in a Saturday morning cup match between London Boys and Glasgow. My mind wasn't really on the job and to cheer myself up on the way back through London to get the train to Aldershot I popped into a public house for a steak and a beer; it was a pub I knew well and was usually full of Orient supporters. They would make me welcome and it would be fun to talk about the 'good old days'.

Not only was the pub full of Orient fans but in the restaurant sat the entire team having their pre-match lunch before an important promotion match. 'Hello Alec, what the hell are you doing here? We thought you would be up in Sheffield'. 'Signing someone are you? Good old Alec, you don't change do you? Even on match days you are still sniffing around.'

I shouldn't have let them go on but I was pleased to see them and, deep down, delighted to hear their banter. And what they were really saying was what I *should* have been doing, what I wanted to be involved with.

My mood was soon shattered when I told them I was only watching Aldershot reserves. 'What for?' they asked. 'What are you doing that for on match day. Fancy that, Alec, you at Aldershot and us battling for promotion.' I left my steak in the end because it only brought home the reality of the situation to me. I wasn't really needed at Arsenal. Why on earth did they approach Orient and ask me to join them in the first place? None of this would have happened.

Arsenal won 8-1 and I didn't see anyone from Aldershot I thought it worth our worrying about. It had been a thoroughly miserable weekend and I felt very sorry for myself.

I knew from that weekend that my break with Arsenal wasn't very far away and, sure enough, it came during training on the Monday morning. As I chatted with the players and began to get ready for action a couple of them came up to me and said there had been a team meeting at Sheffield before Saturday's game.

'We were called to one side and told there was only one boss.' Well there is only one thing you can do in that situation, isn't there? You either fight or go. I was back at Orient in April.

When I look back now I think I made two mistakes over the Arsenal situation. The first was probably joining them in the middle of the season. I should have stayed with Leyton Orient, helped them gain promotion and joined Arsenal on a high and at the start of a new season.

I also think that once I was there I should have taken the job by the scruff of the neck and forced Tom, or whoever it was who didn't really have enough confidence in me, to accept the fact that I was the right man to take charge of playing matters.

And then, if things had still not worked out, I should have stayed and fought hard to put everything right. I thought Ron Atkinson had the right approach when he took over at Manchester United in June 1981. He walked into Old Trafford and said: 'I am the best man for this job.' I thought that was first class, it is the kind of statement that gives directors and supporters immediate confidence in their new manager.

At Highbury I just slipped in without a fuss and soon ended up feeling like a spare part. There were times when I could have kept my lounge suit on instead of changing into a track suit, there just wasn't the involvement I had come to expect and want.

I began to get quite neurotic about the job and at one stage firmly believed that all Arsenal had signed me for was to help to get the best out of Vic Groves. Dear Vic was a super player but he didn't much like training and often had to be persuaded to play. I couldn't get it out of my mind that all Arsenal wanted me for was to get Groves out on the pitch! It sounds stupid now, although little things like that stay in your mind to taunt you when you are mixed up and depressed.

It was also too easy for me to go back to Leyton Orient. The fact that I had a place to go to, a home where they wanted me, made it simple to say to Arsenal 'That's it, I have had enough.'

What I needed was some guidance at that moment in my career. I desperately needed someone to lean on and talk me round. I should have been told 'What the hell are you doing? This is Arsenal, you know, people just don't walk out on a club like that.'

I should have been told to hang on. No one leaves a job after fifty-three days just because it isn't going too well. Wait a little longer and see what happens.

Without that guidance, however, I was a man who had made up his mind. From the moment I decided to resign other things about Arsenal began to worry me. The vastness of Highbury made it an impersonal place and after eight weeks I still met new faces. 'This is not like good old Brisbane Road' I thought to myself all the time. 'You don't belong here Alec, go home.'

On the day I left Arsenal I had arranged to pick Marjorie up at the hairdressers. She knew that all was not well at Highbury but didn't realize that I was going to resign when I had left home after breakfast that morning. I didn't want her to find out so I hid the newspapers I had bought and guided her away from newspaper sellers as we walked arm in arm towards home.

'I have got something to tell you when we get home, luv' I said. 'What have you done now Alec Stock' she replied just as my secret was blown by a seller standing a few yards away. 'Alec Stock sensation' he screamed at the top of his voice. 'Stock resigns, read all about it.' Marjorie looked at me with the kind of expression that wives reserve for husbands at such moments. It is difficult to describe – but no words are needed.

So I left Arsenal, and now at this stage of my career I regret it. I should have stayed and fought for what I really wanted. I had been in management for ten years when Arsenal took me on and when I left I threw all that away.

A lot of people won't understand but I have always been a sensitive old fool and, at the time, I just couldn't work to the best of my ability. Leyton Orient gave me a happy alternative and I took it. Arsenal, however, will go down as one of the great 'might-have-beens' in my life. I still sit at home today and think 'I wonder what I might have achieved as a manager if I had stayed at Arsenal ...' I wonder.

11 Double-crossed in Italy?

There comes a time in every man's life when he asks himself: Where am I going, what do I want to do with my career? It happened to me in the summer of 1957. I was happy at Leyton Orient, we were in the Second Division and were good enough to have a bit of success in the coming season. Indeed I had only been back at the club for fifteen months following my unhappy experience at Arsenal.

At the back of my mind, however, there was a little doubt nagging away, telling me that on the other side of the fence there was more experience, new things to discover. It was urging me to go and explore again. I was probably still a bit upset with myself over the Highbury situation, annoyed that I had let such a marvellous opportunity slip by.

So when my friend Gigi Peronace, Italian football's man in Britain, contacted me for Roma and said that the millionaire Italian First Division club wanted me as their director of training and coaching I saw new horizons opening up in front of my eyes. Was this the new challenge I needed?

Suddenly I realized that the extent of my football knowledge was non-league, Third and Second Division football. I knew the players, managers, grounds, supporters, everything, inside out. The moment Gigi put the phone down I asked myself: 'Have you been around this place too long? What are you going to make of your life?' Or was uprooting the family too much to consider? What do they want me to go to Italy for anyway?

I tossed the problem over in my mind for days, one moment almost deciding to go and the next frightening myself and deciding to sleep on it for another night. The thing that made up my mind for me in the end was that Continental football was getting very fashionable. Everyone was talking about their training and coaching methods.

I realized that if I went for any job with a man who had experience of European football I wouldn't stand a chance of being selected. That was it. I was off to Italy to further my education and give my career a new dimension. I didn't speak a word of Italian but I wanted the challenge of working with Continental players. I rang Gigi and told him 'yes' and handed in my notice to Harry Zussman for the second time in seventeen months.

It was a marvellous compliment to be asked to step from the Second Division into top Italian football. The money was good, the sun shone, the facilities at 'home' were good. 'This is lovely,' I thought to myself every time I woke up in the morning and remembered where I was.

The bonus was that Marjorie liked Italy too. She settled down as soon as she arrived in Rome and that is the biggest hurdle any man can overcome. If your wife is happy in new surroundings then, quite frankly, you should be happy too.

In Italy the pace was very much quicker and the country, the language, and the surroundings took a little longer to get used to. I was delighted that the players responded to me although how my interpreter translated 'It's all about a little thing called pride', during my first meeting with the players, I don't know.

Anyway, respond they did and we lost only one of my first eleven matches. I was getting valuable experience, we played some good old stuff and the reactions of everyone around me seemed to be favourable. 'Lovely, lovely,' I thought. 'This must be going too well.' Old worryguts took over again. 'I wonder what's going to happen?'

It went wrong, totally unexpectedly, one gloriously hot

Sunday when we were playing away to Naples. I had a little routine I went through on Sunday mornings and this day was no exception. After I had driven a couple of players to the ground I borrowed Gigi's car and travelled alone to Rome railway station.

My team and the rest of the party were due at the station a couple of hours later to catch the train to Naples and I used up the time, as usual, reading all the first editions of the English newspapers that had been delivered overnight.

It was something I always looked forward to. A cup of piping-hot coffee, two or three newspapers, and a chance to be alone and put my feet up. I even managed to get an edition of a paper with the results of all my local clubs back in Bath. It was marvellous to sit there every Sunday, reminiscing and reading all about my old clubs.

I have always felt that it is important for a manager to have a few hours on his own, just to think things over in his mind and toss over other problems. I must have looked the typical English tourist sitting on Rome station with the newspapers but it was most enjoyable, lovely.

When I was at Queen's Park Rangers I always used to nip into the local turkish baths at Epsom on Friday afternoons for my couple of hours relaxation. It was usually after I had pinned the team up and I thought I would just let everyone get on with it. If a player wasn't happy he couldn't find me until Saturday morning. I could do a little bit of planning without any distractions. It also helped me to unwind.

My two hours on Rome station always passed too quickly and soon my shadow, the interpreter, and I were strolling along the platform towards the train. I don't know whether it was because I was so relaxed and not really concentrating but I suddenly realized that we were just about to get on the wrong train. 'This is not right,' I told him. 'I didn't use this platform and train when I took the reserves to Naples last week'.

I still don't know if that was a genuine mistake, although it did mean we missed the correct train and my players went off without me. I was very annoyed because punctuality is one of the things I pride myself on. I can't remember ever being late for a match, appointment, interview, meeting, anything. It put me in the wrong frame of mind.

We eventually arrived at the Naples ground and my preparation went from bad to worse when, with one and half hours to go to the kick-off, the club announced that the team had been changed; the centre forward I had selected, Swedish international Gunnar Nordahl, was being replaced by an eighteen-year-old boy, Alfredo Orlando.

Technical Manager Antonio Buzini and I had had our differences of opinion over certain things since I arrived in Italy and yet there just didn't seem any justification for this decision that he had announced so unexpectedly. The irony of it was that I had stopped the club selling Orlando only a few days before the game. I had to plead with them, 'Please don't sell, he is going to be a great player. This one is for us.'

So again I saw people as they really were. I smelt disloyalty again in my career and refused to accept the decision with a smile. As I have already explained, and I hope proved, I will never be a yes-man in soccer. My team had been beaten only once in eleven matches and there was just no point in changing the side.

When a manager's decisions are questioned he can do one of three things. He can fight it, accept it and never have complete control again, or get out. I suppose some managers would say: 'That's OK, do what you like and just keep sending down the money.' They would just sit tight and wait for things to sort themselves out. But I have never been like that.

I asked myself at the time whether it was all a complete put-up job. The wrong train, arriving late at Naples and not being around for the full preparation on match day gave someone at Roma the chance to say I had unjustifiably abandoned my team. That was nonsense. I have never turned my back on players in my life.

The damage was done as far as I was concerned and Roma and I could never have been the same after that. I still don't understand why someone somewhere inside the club wanted to upset the applecart; life can get so complicated at times it is difficult to follow and understand people. To me one defeat out of eleven matches was not a bad old record and, quite frankly, it had gone better than I expected. It's just another part of my life that will remain a mystery, another puzzle that will stay unsolved.

It would be interesting now to gather all the people I haven't understood around me in one room and ask them why, what did you do it for, why on earth did you spoil something so exciting? On reflection that would not be such a good idea, perhaps I would find the answers too frustrating and annoying. It would probably only make my regrets even more bitter.

That Sunday in Naples certainly ruined what I thought was going to be a happy and long career in Italian football. It was not long before I returned to England. There to greet me, as always, was Leyton Orient chairman, Harry Zussman. For the third time he opened the door to Brisbane Road for me. 'We will have him back' he said and after much soul searching I went back in March 1958, less than a year after I had gone to Italy.

I suppose it is easy now to say that it was a mistake to return a third time but I was out of work and Leyton Orient still meant an awful lot to me. When I eventually made the final break a year later it had to be for good. I had to do something more with my career although I still didn't know quite what. At that stage I still didn't know what was in store for me.

12 The Old Victorian Lady

The trouble with me is that I always got the sack or left a club at my peak. Just when I thought to myself 'Alec Stock you have done well here', everything would blow up in my face and I would be sent hurtling back to square one.

I was sacked by Roma and Queen's Park Rangers and walked out on Arsenal, Luton and Fulham, all at times when I should have been making the final push for a little bit of glory. My romance with Luton ended after the Vehicle and General collapse and subsequent boardroom reshuffle; the end at Fulham came after the biggest boardroom bust-up I have experienced.

When I led Fulham out for the 1975 FA Cup Final it was beyond my wildest dreams that a year and a half later I would be walking away from Craven Cottage. After Wembley I honestly thought that at the age of fifty-eight I had found contentment for the rest of my career. I said to Marjorie a couple of days after the dust had settled on the Final, 'This job will see me out.'

And see me out it did. In December 1976 I was happy to turn my back on a club that had lost its image. My nickname for Fulham had always been 'The Old Victorian Lady'. A club with a bit of style and class. Now it's just a rough old working-class chap.

Every manager of a club should know, and indeed be told, what is happening at his club. The playing side is of course his main concern although I believe he should be kept informed at all times about money and the general running of the club.

At Fulham I gradually lost that all-important feeling of being 'in the picture' until at the end I didn't have a clue what the club wanted or, indeed, where we were going. It was a very sad and sudden change-round.

The first sniff of a new era came when a lovely old boy and the club's vice chairman called 'Chappie' D'Amato died. Chappie was Fulham through and through, he loved the place and was one of the people who made the club different. He was a character, and stuck up for the club through thick and thin. He was only interested in one thing and that was making Fulham better. When he died I never thought there was anyone around with influence who would stick up for Fulham Football Club. Chappie was not interested in himself, only the image of the club he loved.

His death was the first seed of doubt sown in my mind and then came a mystery that I will never understand as long as I live. I wish Tommy Trinder, the comedian chairman of Fulham whom I honestly believe loved everything about the club, would explain to me and a lot of other people why he sold his shares to Sir Eric Miller.

I would like to know why it happened, how it happened, and whether it was really necessary. One thing is sure, once Tommy made his last appearance on the Fulham stage the place was never the same again. Other directors resigned with him or soon after and before my eyes the club had been turned on its head. Tommy no doubt has his reasons although I could never understand why, in the late 1970s when football clubs were such a valuable property to have in your control, he should sell out.

I have talked about loyalty a lot in this book and I thought that was disappointing to me, turning his back suddenly on the people he had employed and worked closely with. Maybe he knew what was coming.

Once more we return to people and their qualities. Sir Eric Miller was another mystery man to me. I never really understood him or got close to him. And I just couldn't tell you how much power he had in the club, or how much love for it. The fact that he didn't go to Wembley for Fulham's FA Cup Final or the celebration banquet afterwards answered a few of my fears.

Fulham at Wembley. You would walk there from the other side of the country, wouldn't you, if you were totally involved? It just had to be the greatest day in anyone's life if they happened to be director, president, chairman, and true supporter of a Second Division club who had got to Wembley for the first time. From that day on I thought 'You belong but you don't really care.'

Although Fulham didn't play well at Wembley I always thought that the structure of the club was sound and the team was good enough to see us through a few more seasons. There were also some good young players coming through the youth policy and, quite frankly, there was no need for any sudden collapse or take-over or panic.

At a club like Fulham there are always financial pressures and, like at most smaller clubs, the manager knows he is going to have to sell occasionally to keep his club's nose above water. Fulham was no exception and there was pressure surrounding payment for the 'Eric Miller grand-stand' but I never really worried about that. I have always wheeled and dealed the transfer market with success.

To help give everyone a lift after Wembley we signed George Best and Rodney Marsh. I thought that the crowd, who still had not responded to success and the other players, would welcome two of the biggest names in the country with open arms.

The other players, I think and hope, enjoyed having Best and Marsh around although the season continued to be far too inconsistent for my liking. One day the crowd would respond and we would be brilliant, with our two big names turning it on, the next Saturday we would lose and a few more fans would disappear.

It was an in-and-out season. We would win well, draw and then go a couple of games without getting a point. Then, alas, the novelty of Best and Marsh began to wear off, although at times you wonder what exactly the Fulham public want these days.

We gave them success and a Wembley Cup Final and immediately introduced a little bit of glamour and style. I thought it was a nice throwback to the days when the locals would turn up to see a few characters in the team like Macedo, Langley, Lowe, Cook, Haynes and Chamberlin. I thought they would come in their thousands to watch three of the biggest names in football, Moore, Marsh and Best. Sadly, we just couldn't hold their interest.

I am delighted to be able to say, however, that during my career I have worked with George Best. He is undoubtedly the finest player I have seen and it was marvellous just to watch him in training. He would do things that would make the other players just stop and watch him in pure admiration.

The only problem with George was that we never quite knew where he was. He sometimes just turned up on his own in the afternoon for training and then slipped off without saying much about anything.

While he was with us he was selected again for Northern Ireland and, with his co-operation, we arranged a press conference at the ground for 11 a.m. A lot of press boys were there, television, radio and even a few Northern Ireland correspondents had flown over for the occasion. One snag, we couldn't find George. I sent Ted Drake out in a taxi looking for him. We knew he had a flat in Chelsea but he wasn't there. Ted, much to our embarrassment and frustration, returned empty handed. The press conference was cancelled and we wondered if the club would ever see George again.

At 2 p.m. he strolled into the ground and showed complete surprise when there was no one there to greet him. And that was Best, unpredictable, annoying, an enigma. But so brilliant with a ball at his feet. And there was no way Fulham or I were going to change him at that stage of his career. He came, flirted with football and Fulham for a little while, and then disappeared. It is one of the sad stories of football, of course, but there will always be a place in my memories for the little Irishman.

One of Sir Eric Miller's last acts for Fulham Football Club was to introduce Ernie Clay to the board. I have already made known my feelings for Mr Clay and the club was definitely never the same from the moment he arrived. That is purely my opinion; others will no doubt say that Clay is the best thing that has happened to Fulham.

All I have ever been interested in is football and running a club to the best of my ability. The players and the team come first in my eyes although it is important to balance things out throughout the club. At Fulham I had to start fighting little battles that had nothing to do with football.

The board meetings became talk-ins to revolutionize the game. All I have ever wanted to do was sit down with directors and talk about how to improve my club, not how to change the world. Those Fulham directors were so new, beginners at the game, I wondered how they could start so ambitiously. 'What do you know about it?' I would ask them. 'I have had more experience than all of you put together.' They were people who wanted to be seen for reasons over and above a football club. And, most of the time, they talked nonsense.

Once again I return to my fears about chairmen and directors. Are the new men at Craven Cottage really interested in the future of their club? A football club is a very delicate piece of machinery, if you tinker about with it and throw a big spanner in the works it takes an awful long time to repair.

You just can't rock the boat overnight and expect to get it back on course straight away. I always knew that I would have to sell to keep the club afloat but in the end I just couldn't take any more. So I bailed out.

After a heated exchange with Ernie Clay I knew that Fulham were about to be added to my list of past clubs. Bobby Campbell, the man I brought in to replace Bill Taylor, and very much a Clay follower, was put in charge of the team. That put me in no man's land although a number of officials asked me to stay as a consultant. 'What do I want to do that for?' I asked. 'I am a football manager. That is what I am good at.' I wish Fulham well in the future of course. Malcolm Macdonald is manager there now and he will work hard to get them back where they belong.

My handling of Bill Taylor is another little regret in my life. His work at Fulham won him recognition with England and I knew one day that he and I would have to part company. Taylor impressed former England manager Don Revie during the 1980 World Cup Finals in West Germany with his thoroughness and knowledge.

It wasn't long before Revie contacted me to invite Taylor into the England set-up as a coach and I am delighted that he has stayed to work alongside Ron Greenwood. Bill however never really wanted to leave Fulham and I had to persuade him to go to Manchester City when Tony Book offered him the job as first team coach. Should I have let him stay? I don't know. I thought it was progress for him, an obvious step up.

Fulham today are firmly in the power of Ernie Clay. In four years he has won control of a London football club and believe me that is not bad going. Hence my fears of the club owner. But that is the man, he likes to be seen and heard, no matter what. He has introduced Rugby League to Fulham and football and in many ways that does represent progress. I wouldn't like to guess what his next step will be but you can be sure that something will always be happening when Mr Ernie Clay is around.

It's just that he wasn't for me. I couldn't work with him and that is why in December 1976 I left Fulham. It took a lot of doing. My immediate reaction was to think of Luton a few years earlier and how that empire had fallen in front of my eyes. Just like Fulham, I never expected to leave Luton so abruptly when we were going along so smoothly.

That collapse started on a golfing holiday in Jersey. The team deserved a break and I was looking forward to a few days' rest. I had worked flat out for months, clocking up enough hours and miles to make anyone exhausted. On the first night in Jersey I had gone to bed early and was having a lie-in, something I never managed to do at Luton when I was driving up the M1 every morning. I had the papers, a pot of tea and life was marvellous. I smiled to myself as I nestled back for an hour's read.

The first headline in the *Daily Telegraph* hit me between the eyes like a sledgehammer. 'V and G collapse.' I just held my head in my hands for I knew exactly what that meant to the club and me. Life would never be the same again at Kenilworth Road.

We needed to win our next game, on the Tuesday night at Bristol City, to keep up our push for promotion from the Second Division. We were 2-0 up and coasting when, in the last ten minutes, Bristol City scored three times.

It was a freak result, a situation that hadn't been possible for eighty minutes. And when the referee blew the final whistle a million things started to go through my mind and the thing that kept returning was that a sign had been put on Luton Town and Alec Stock again. Was I not supposed to get to the First Division?

'It has been decreed that we shouldn't,' I kept saying to myself, and by the next morning I knew what was coming. I had made up my mind that, for a while, Luton were on the slippery slope. Macdonald was sold, other players wanted to go once they saw Malcolm's deal and the glory he was getting in the First Division, we missed promotion and the board split apart. It seemed to happen very quickly.

I was very distressed when my Luton side had to be changed. It was a most excellent young team and so rewarding to Harry Haslam, Jimmy Andrews and I because it was built from nothing. When you watched them running around in training you thought to yourself: 'What a bunch of smoothies, I fancy us to do something this year.' I had a feeling that once the final piece of the jigsaw was complete we would go places together. Had it not been for the V and G collapse I believe Luton would be in the First Division today. With Alec Stock as manager?

There was a marvellous mixture of talent and hard work,

and experience and youth. Men like Mike Keen, my captain whom I signed from Queen's Park Rangers, and Alan Slough, who teamed up with me at Fulham. They are the kind of reliable characters that every club and manager needs.

If you told Keen and Slough that we were training in Timbuktu tomorrow they would be there first, waiting for you to arrive on the training ground. I was delighted when Millwall contacted me in the summer of 1981 and asked me if I thought that Slough would do a good job as youth team coach. I am sure he has got a big future in the game.

I certainly couldn't call my life in football management drab, could I? There haven't been many dull days and I can honestly say that I have enjoyed most of them. There are people I haven't got on with and that is part and parcel of every job, and situations that have been very frustrating. My relationship with players has always been marvellous and there are incidents I look back on now and wonder how they happened and how we survived them.

At Queen's Park Rangers you couldn't have picked a more mixed bag if you had tried and my heart went out to them one Christmas when we were due to play away to Plymouth Argyle on Boxing Day morning. I don't know how the computer came up with that one but it only meant one thing, we had to travel on Christmas Day. I started to hunt around for the best travel arrangements and how we could arrange lunch for the players during the journey.

Lunch, in fact, proved the biggest problem. No one wanted to open up on Christmas Day just to feed a bunch of hungry footballers. The press got hold of the news of our predicament and after a couple of stories appeared I received a letter from a farmer in Yeovil. It was an invitation for us to join him and his family for Christmas Day lunch.

It was a marvellous gesture although I had my doubts and I rang our friendly farmer and told him 'You know what you are letting yourself in for, don't you? There are sixteen of us and the players will eat your farm for you. These blokes are hungry fellas.'

He insisted and I wish now I had taken a camera with me

on that Christmas Day. I would have used up a film. You should have seen my players, all sitting around the table with the farmer, his wife and their children. There were paper hats, balloons, streamers, it was beautiful. Then at four o'clock in the afternoon I had to pinch myself hard to make sure I wasn't dreaming. Out in the garden stood Marsh and Sanderson, paper hats on and double brandies in hand, teaching the children a few tricks. Well, what can you do in a situation like that? You just let them get on with it, don't you. Can't spoil a party, even if there is an important game in the morning. The players loved it, the kids loved it and yes, I loved it too. And just to round off a smashing little trip we beat Plymouth! Not a bad old life, is it. Hmmm.

It wasn't such a good Christmas Day a few seasons earlier when we actually had to play on 25 December. We found ourselves at Liverpool, another great little piece of fixture arranging. 'It's not too bad, fellas,' I told the players. 'At least it's a morning kick-off, we will be home for tea.'

We hadn't bargained for a train dispute and at three in the afternoon we were still waiting on Wigan station. The buffet was closed, we had lost 0-1 and my goalkeeper had his arm in a sling with a broken shoulder. Tea? It was supper before we slumped into our homes. Happy Christmas!

It is the happy times, of course, that you always remember and at the end of a career you look back with affection on the hundreds of people you made friends with. I have also talked long and hard in this book about the people I have fallen out with. But I don't believe that you make enemies in football; the game is a huge collection of people and inevitably there are many you are not going to understand or want to work with.

That is what has happened to me. I also like to think I can still go up to these people and say: 'You were wrong and you made a complete mess of that.' Football is all about opinions and these are mine. They, no doubt, have their own and if the day ever comes when we can't meet over a beer and talk about the past and the future then there is no real hope for the game.

13 Buying and Selling

Being poor makes you choosey. That has been my way of life in football management. I have never had much money to spend; instead I have relied on a mixture of judgment, luck and bargains.

For a manager who has the reputation of a wheeler-dealer and someone who has bought and sold more players than most it will come as a surprise to a lot of people that I have never really enjoyed playing the transfer market. Going out to buy worries me like mad.

I am better, and certainly get more satisfaction, out of finding my own players for nothing and developing them into first team players. When other managers have said to me in the past, 'I have just signed so and so for £75,000 as a squad player', I open my eyes in amazement. I have never been able to buy fringe players. They have all had to be just right for the job – and cheap.

I have lived through the million pound era and yet my record signing is still the £80,000 I paid Charlton Athletic, as Fulham manager in July 1972, for centre half Paul Went. That is an indication of the basement buying I have done over the years.

Selling, of course, is different. It is the easiest part of football management. It is not clever to sell, you can get rid of good players every day of the week. You may be able to manipulate a few more quid out of a club before the deal is done, and even that is not hard. If a club wants a player badly they will shake your hand off if the price is right. Malcolm Macdonald was my prime example. Newcastle were not going to take no for an answer and they were not even put off by my overnight request for 'another £30,000'.

I can't say I have missed being able to buy international players at the peak of their careers or going out with a million in my pocket to spend on one player. I have never experienced that situation and, quite frankly, it still doesn't seem right to me.

The ideal club set-up is something like Ipswich. I would certainly have liked to have been manager there as they have worked hard to enjoy the best of both worlds. Bobby Robson can buy big in the market when the player he feels is right for him is available. And he has the backing of a very virile and productive youth policy. Ron Grey, Robson's chief scout, has done a marvellous job at Portman Road.

Bobby has also proved himself a good bargain hunter and the Dutchmen, Frank Thijssen and Arnold Muhren, were two exceptional signings when the deals in this country were going through the roof. I was very proud of him with those signings, they were my kind of deals.

To me the most beautiful thing in football has always been to find someone who has been rejected by many others, work hard with him, and then watch him develop into a first team player. You can sit back then with tremendous satisfaction and say 'There is a little bit of me out there. That is our product.' Your judgment has been right all the way down the line. The one who gave me most satisfaction was Frank Sibley, a teenager we signed for Queen's Park Rangers when everyone else warned me to be careful.

Frank had struggled with his health as a boy and many people never dreamt that he would make a professional footballer. But we took him after watching a junior trial game and did everything we could to develop him as a player. By the time he was seventeen, Frank was an important part of the first team. Playing alongside the centre half he was quite the best kid I found for anyone. A sensational player. It was lovely to see him make it.

When I returned to Queen's Park Rangers as a director following my bust-up with Fulham, Frank was the manager at Loftus Road and, it seemed, doing a fair job. It broke my heart when he decided to quit and I tried for days to persuade him to stay. When I last heard of him he was coaching a non-League side and working away from football during the day. What a waste! Little gold nuggets like him were never easy to find because my clubs, Orient, Queen's Park Rangers, Luton and Fulham, were never the top attraction for boys wanting to make their name in football.

We would move in when the big boys had creamed off the schoolboy internationals and other stars of tomorrow they wanted. It made finding someone like Sibley even more satisfying. Paying out small amounts for other discards and rejected players and turning them into bigger and better fish was just as rewarding. Marsh and Macdonald were the big captures and there were others just as important to us.

My very good scout at Queen's Park Rangers, Derek Healey, asked me one day to go and take a look at a boy called Dennis Bond playing for Walthamstow Boys in a Junior Cup Final. Bond was outstanding but we discovered he was already committed to Watford. So I looked again during the second half and Derek and I decided to take a little gamble on a couple of brothers called Ian and Roger Morgan playing on the wing, a hard working midfield kid Mick Leach and another youngster named Derek Belloti.

That is just a little slice of luck you always need. We couldn't get the one we went for so instead took four more and, after much hard work, they all made it. Roger Morgan, of course, went to Spurs for £110,000 on 7 February 1969.

Another schoolboy we discovered was a little midfield dynamo called Alan Glover. He cost us nothing and later the club sold him to West Brom for £70,000. Lovely little deals, aren't they? It's surely what the transfer market is all about.

Buying and selling has always been a team effort in my clubs. I have always had staff around whom I trusted and would never have dreamt of signing or selling someone without getting their opinion. What a dreadful state of affairs if your coach picks up his morning paper and finds that the club have sold someone he has been working with for years?

I have made a daily habit of sitting down with my coach over a cup of tea for half an hour and talking about the club. We may discuss tactics, money, players, anything. It is very important to involve everyone and make them feel they're very much part of the set-up.

There is no way a manager is always right and many times I have been guided or persuaded away from a player or situation I had set up. If you don't give other people authority and ask them to involve themselves, you only end up with chaos.

Whenever I have appointed staff I have always gone for men with ideas and a strong personality. I have always liked to think I could rely on them when the situation arose. Secretaries can help in this department too. They are always on the end of the telephone and often hear of players being made available. So they are brought in as well; John Smith at Orient pointed me in the direction of a couple of deals.

Your coach may not always agree with you, of course, and quite frankly in those situations the manager must have the last say. If your right-hand man says 'I don't fancy it' when you mention a possible signing, the answer has been to explain that Jim Smith is the best we can get and afford. 'We will just have to make him better.'

At the bottom end of the market there are two types of player available and it is all to do with attitude. The first man, who has been rejected and transfer listed, knows that he has got to change. You talk to him and say 'It's not been going quite right, has it? But don't worry, we want you and you can do this for us. But you have got to change. This is how we do things here.'

He responds and gets better and a few weeks later, when he is enjoying himself for the first time for quite a long time, he comes to see you and says: 'Thanks boss, I'll not look back now.' That kind of player is a turn-up for the book, a real bonus.

The other guy signs for you and promises to change. He

says he will and things look good for a few matches. Then he reverts to his old bad habits and you can understand why he was sold in the first place. That is a real kick in the teeth. You know you have made a bad signing.

The one aspect of signing a player and working with him on which I have prided myself is that I have brought them up well. It's a strong point of mine and it stems from pride. I like players to look and dress well. They are professionals and should act like it.

Most kids from working-class backgrounds who come into football on the bottom rung have nothing. That is not an insult, it is the truth. I like to think that some of them who have passed under my control have matured into something better. We have changed a few characters over the years and that pleases me no end.

Boys have got to want to learn, of course, and once they have discovered good habits they are easier to work with. If a person wants to improve, the man (coach) doing the teaching has got half of his job done. Most of my players have been brought up to like to play. They have enjoyed themselves.

Playing football is really a very selfish sport. I tell kids today that every lap they run, every ball they kick and bit of sweat they drop, is for them and for no one else. They are not losing seven pounds in a training session for me, it's for them. To help them become better players, and hopefully, better people.

Stuart Leary, the old Kent cricketer who was not a bad old player for us at Queen's Park Rangers, had a bit of style and pride. He was a good example to everyone around him and I remember Mark Lazarus saying to me a couple of weeks after I signed him for the first time, 'I'd like to be like him one day' pointing at Leary.

I first signed Mark Lazarus for Queen's Park Rangers in September 1960 for £3,000. It was the start of a superb relationship and I took him back on two other occasions. I sold him when the offer was too good to turn down and signed him again when I needed a winner with a bit of ability. Mark would just say to me: 'Give me a few more quid a week Alec, and I'll be back.' Lovely, lovely. Those kind of deals I like.

A year later I sold him to Wolves for £26,000. It was the biggest transfer of Mark's career and Mrs Lazarus turned up at the ground to make sure that 'all was well' with the deal. When Mark and his wife came into the boardroom to meet Wolves manager, Stan Cullis, and a couple of his directors, Mrs Lazarus was carrying a big wide handbag.

I leaned over to my chairman George Woodhouse and whispered 'George, you know why she has got that big bag? It's to put all the readies in!' Little did we know that was almost the truth. Just before Mark signed his contract his wife interrupted and spoke to Cullis. 'Now listen' she said, 'If you think you are signing my Mark for £26,000 and he is only getting £250 out of it, you have another think coming!' I thought that was beautiful and couldn't hide my amusement. 'Well played my girl,' I thought. 'I would double your housekeeping.'

Mark was soon back with me for a reduced fee and I sold him again, this time to Brentford for £12,000 in January 1964. Just over a year and a half later he was back, God bless him, signed for £7,000 and stayed to become a vital member of our League Cup Final and promotion triumph. We parted company for the last time when I sold him to another London club, Crystal Palace, and there will always be a place in my heart for Mark Lazarus. He would run through a wall for me, and often did!

I think he was grateful that I gave his life some meaning in the shape of professional football. He made a couple of bob and was a smashing bloke to have around. Very good for morale. He was grateful to me and I was delighted with the mileage I clocked out of him. It was a good partnership.

These are the kind of people and the kind of deals I have always worked hard on. They are so rewarding. There is a lot of luck, of course, attached to transfers. Being in the right place, spotting a player when you are looking at someone else, talking to a manager when he has just popped one of his players you have fancied for years on the transfer list.

Stan Berry, my chief scout at Orient, who lived in the lovely Surrey village of Claygate, discovered more players than most. He once persuaded me to travel to Shrewsbury to watch a couple of kids he thought had a good future. I was a very reluctant traveller because I was due to play cricket on that particular day. 'It will be worth your while, Alec, they are good.' 'It had better be Stan' I replied. He was right as usual and within six months they both had Welsh caps. Cyril Lea and Mal Lucas, two little goldmines.

Other managers had a little saying about Berry that summed him up nicely. 'Alec, we don't mind your scout having a look at my player but when he rubs their backs down when they get out of the shower, that is a bit strong.'

I have always gone for London-based players as I have already explained, and the only man from outside the capital on my books at Queen's Park Rangers when we had our glory season in 1967 was Keith Sanderson, a tough Yorkshireman whom I signed for £6,000 from Malcolm Allison at Plymouth Argyle.

Sanderson was a part-timer, had a degree and was hard as they come. I knew that if we went out in front the opposition would have to tread all over Keith Sanderson to win the game. Rodney would wear them down with his skill and goals and Keith would make sure we didn't lose.

If things were not going well in the first half and a certain player, I thought, was not pulling his weight, I knew that I wouldn't have to say much at half-time. Sanderson was already there, crouching over the player, foaming at the mouth with effort and shaking his fist in the culprit's face. 'You are trying to lose me money' he would scream.

One of the best deals I did as far as value for money was concerned came after I sold Luton's Bruce Rioch and his brother Neil to Tommy Docherty at Aston Villa for £110,000. With the cash we bought Macdonald for £18,000, Keen (£17,500), John Collins (£10,000), and Matt Tees (£25,000) and still had some money to spare.

A couple of seasons later we struck lucky again when Harry Haslam and I went up to Old Trafford to take a look at a winger called Jim Ryan. He was good and we also liked another of United's reserves, Don Givens. So we persuaded United to sell them both to us for £32,000. We thought that was another good deal and United were quite happy. Givens went on to form a superb partnership with Macdonald, and Luton eventually sold him to Queen's Park Rangers, at a big profit of course.

Luton played against Halifax in August 1969 and although we won convincingly a big centre half kept getting in the way of everything we tried to do. I inquired the next day and Alan Ball senior said he was for sale at £30,000. So Chris Nicholl joined us and started off on a successful career. He was sold to Aston Villa in March 1972 for £90,000 and Chris is now with Southampton having gained a number of caps for Northern Ireland along the way.

Harry and I were still studying the Fulham throw-away list and we picked up two more incredible bargains. They gave full back John Ryan a free transfer and put a tough-tackling player called Don Shanks on the open-to-offer list. We took them both. Shanks did a good job for me before he was sold to QPR. In 1981 he made a free transfer to Brighton and proved to be an excellent first Division defender.

Now I look back, an awful lot of good players passed through my hands at Luton. Viv Busby was picked up for £300 from Wycombe, Peter Anderson we discovered playing non-League football for Hendon. Even Derek Hales was captured for £2,000 from Dartford. I always feel sorry for a coach called Theo Foley when I think of Hales and his former partner at Charlton, Mike Flanagan. Theo worked so hard with them both at Charlton but was then sacked, and from the outside saw his two protégés transferred for almost a million pounds, Hales to Derby and Flanagan to Crystal Palace.

The extraordinary thing about selling players is that the man you have sold suddenly becomes the favourite of the crowd and the directors. People ask you 'Why did you sell him?' and letters appear on your desk calling you all the names under the sun for negotiating such a deal.

At Fulham I once sold Paul Went to Portsmouth and centre forward Steve Earle to Leicester in the space of a couple of days and got a terrible reaction. My critics didn't think before they spoke, however, and if they had analysed the situation first they would have discovered that it was a good double deal.

We had John Lacy coming through and ready to take Went's place in the team and when Jimmy Bloomfield offered me £90,000 for Earle that was just too good to turn down. I knew I could get Busby from Luton and Earle was keen to go, he needed a change after being at Fulham for a number of years. The deal did both him and the club a good turn.

Supporters must realize that managers only sell players for the good of the club. No manager in the country wants to sell his best men. It is the easiest part of the job and certainly the cruellest. Selling can also put a manager under tremendous pressure; the pressure of finding a replacement and, in some cases, the worry of actually being paid all the money for the player he has just sold.

Most transfers throughout football have always been done on the 'never-never' basis. Ever since I did my first deal, straight cash transfers have been a rarity. There just isn't the money around, especially today when up to almost two million pounds is changing hands. The norm is so much down and the rest paid over an agreed period.

The biggest problem arising from such a transaction is that your supporters immediately start asking 'What is he going to do with the money? Who is he going to buy?' They don't realize that you have only got half to play with and usually a big chunk of that is pumped straight back into the club.

I have never been entirely happy with the 'small print' rules of the never-never transfer. The paybacks are purely an agreement between the two clubs and I have always thought that the Football League should have more of an official say. I was surprised and disappointed when a rule to ensure that paybacks were completed by a certain period was tossed out at the League's seminar in 1981. Why not rule that all outstanding money is paid back by the end of the same season?

It would have stopped managers worrying whether the balance would actually be paid. On a number of occasions I have known managers and chairmen pluck up enough courage to ask 'Can we have our money, it is overdue.' It is a nagging pressure you could do without, especially after letting a player go whom you know will be hard to replace. There is not a man in the game who doesn't sit down and ask himself 'Was it a mistake?' after selling.

There are some clubs, of course, who prefer to pay cash, especially when the price is not too high. Jim Gregory was always very good in the transfer market. If you wanted a player and Jim agreed, the deal would be over in a few hours. There was no messing about with Jim. 'Let's show them we mean business' he would say to me. It makes life very easy. I can remember the surprise on Bill Nicholson's face when we went to sign Les Allen from Tottenham. Bill was obviously expecting the usual money down and repayments deal. Jim just pulled out his chequebook and wrote out a cheque for £21,000.

One decision the League did make for the 1981 season was the return to the loan system of transfers and I must say that I am still a bit against this. I fear that some managers may abuse the rule for their own good.

When the loan system was first introduced it was good, because it meant that managers were able to give junior players experience. I always thought that was just about the right mood of the thing. Now a loan deal can decide promotion and relegation and, quite frankly, that stinks a bit to me.

I can't see why a manager should be able to loan players right up to a couple of months before the end of the season when he suddenly realizes that he needs an experienced striker to play alongside his kids or a midfield anchor man to 'tighten things up' and make sure points are not dropped.

There is also the distasteful situation when managers help their friends out. Jim Smith owes Bill Brown a favour so he loans him a player; and that might just keep his team in the First Division. Surely that can't be good for the game. The loan transfer system definitely needs looking at once more.

I thought the League should have made the deadline for loan deals before Christmas instead of transfer deadline day in March. I would have thought that managers could have made up their minds before then.

Although I have never had money to burn in the market I know that my reaction to international stars and million pound players would have to be the same. I have treated players as equals all through my career and could never imagine putting on an act for someone just because he was a household name.

I have always sat down with men I want to sign and quietly told them what I expect from them; our standards, rules. 'We take a bit of pride in ourselves here' I tell them. 'I hope to make you a better player and if you work hard you are going to have a cracking living.' It's common sense really and if a player doesn't respond you know he is not worth signing anyway.

It was marvellous to sign Bobby Moore and Alan Mullery and, quite frankly, they were a little exception to my signing rules. They had chosen Fulham as the club they wanted to play for at the end of their careers and we were delighted to have them. We were proud, it was a big day for Fulham.

We didn't go into raptures over them, just made them aware how delightful it was they had chosen Fulham. They gave the place a bit of style and that is what I was looking for.

The thing I admired most about them both was that they were no trouble. Once they had signed a contract they stuck to it. They never banged on my door asking for more money and you never heard them say a bad word about the club. It was beautiful and for a while I was a very contented man. Everything was just right.

It was delightful to see them abroad. They were ambassadors of the club, English football and the youngsters in my side responded to them.

Moore was calm, cool; he commanded respect just by turning up. Mullery was his ideal foil, more demanding in public, a motivator and Fulham through and through. If a player had not responded to something in the dressing-room I would know that Mullery would put things right on the pitch. Sure enough, after a couple of minutes that player had felt the wrath of Mullery's tongue. 'If you don't like it here and you don't want to play for Fulham you know what you can do' he would tell them. It makes you wonder what players like Moore and Mullery would command on the transfer market today. Now you really are talking about class. Not like some of today's so-called superstars who are up for auction at the moment under the infamous Freedom of Contract agreement.

Three years ago I stood up at a South East Counties Dinner and said 'Gentlemen, the transfer market is about to go through the roof. Please don't be surprised if very soon we have the million pound player.' I was shouted down, they all thought I was mad. Yet it was easy to see that something outrageous was going to happen, the market had no guide-lines, it was all over the place.

There is a similar outcry today that the 'bottom has fallen out of the market' and the moans are coming directly from the managers and people who allowed it to happen. Who made it fall apart? Who frightened most of us to death? They did.

Now we must all wait and see what happens and pray that some sanity returns to the transfer market. Freedom of Contract has lifted the market almost out of the hands of managers, and the players are now in the driving seat. It is the players who can dictate the future shape of the game at the top. What we must hope for is that they have a bit of style and pride in the game. If they only think of themselves then we are about to take another giant step backwards.

The secret of a good manager has always been good buying. Now, going shopping is made even harder by Freedom of Contract. Last season I asked a manager if so and so was available and he answered: 'I'm not sure, you had better ask him.' Is that good for the game? Maybe I'm too old-fashioned but I have always liked doing deals with other managers and have then looked after the players' interests.

Perhaps managers should put away the chequebook for a while and turn the clock back a few years and go looking for kids and bargains. You don't have to buy big to be successful – I hope I have proved that in my own way.

No, I have never been a top manager but I have survived on a shoestring and some fair old players have passed through me during my career. I can't believe that there aren't any more to discover.

14 Coaching

Les Gore, my number two at Orient, got only one instruction from me at the start of every season. 'OK Les, you know what I want, prepare them. Same as usual, hmmm. Turn me out a team that is fit.'

Simple. Or so we thought. Les was my trainer and it was his job to make sure that the players were ready for each match. It was not a lot to ask and Les was damn good at it.

If I gave such an instruction to my colleague today, he would look at me in complete amazement. For he is no longer a trainer. He is the coach, a man of tactics and method and a language that, quite frankly, I often fail to understand. I am sure that the English dictionary has been rewritten for coaches. Their jargon is now a marvellous piece of invention, containing words I never thought I would have heard related to a game that is basically not very complicated.

I have never employed anyone to simply work with the players. I have always wanted to be involved with tactics. And the way my team played has, without question, been a combination of ideas.

Players should also be involved. After all they know if the team is good enough to operate in a certain way or carry off a fresh idea that the management has come up with. Players are very important, never forget that if you are a modern coach.

Captains and senior players have always been part of my

discussion group which decides just how we are going to perform. I was furious with the criticism England manager Ron Greenwood received during the 1981 Home International Championships when he admitted that he had discussed how to beat Scotland with his players, and consequently dropped West Bromwich Albion winger Peter Barnes.

It is not a crime to talk to your players and accusations of player power are utter nonsense. I have used players' knowledge all through my career. If someone has got a better idea than you, why not use it? Greenwood, I feel, can't win with certain critics and people in the game. He admitted after that Scotland match that he felt he was being belted on the chin every day and I know exactly what he meant. You are so exposed and open to criticism.

I'm not sure who invented the job of football coach although it sounds like something from the Walter Winterbottom era of thirty years ago. All I know is that I suddenly discovered that 'coaching' was the 'in' thing during the summer months.

Like most managers then I always found the summers a bit of a strain. It was the time of the year when wages had to be found and you knew you had to stay close to the ground in case a player became available or the bank manager wanted to know how much was being paid in that week. Would it cover the bills? Management was, and still is, a twenty-four-hour job. You can never let go.

Then it happened, right in front of our eyes and without managers being able to do much about it. Our trainers, number twos, assistants began to float away in the summer for something called a 'coaching course'. It had the complete backing of the Football Association despite many raised eyebrows at the start.

I voiced my opinion long, hard and often. 'You ought to do something about management. We are important, we are the backbone of this game.' We didn't really want to stop it, we just didn't know if it was completely necessary. I still don't.

Coaching, of course, is now a huge part of the modern game. There are hundreds of them, all with different ideas, all talking their own kind of language.

I have looked long and hard at coaching in the last few years and often ask myself: Do we have too many, are there enough fresh ideas and do these people really care about the effect they can have on the game? Do they always want to improve the image of the game or are they playing out their own little fantasies?

If you analyse the job, what makes a good coach? And how, I want to know, does he become qualified after a couple of weeks away on one of these courses? The fact that he has got a badge surely doesn't mean that he is ready and able to work with the best.

On the Continent there are degrees of coaching you must go through before you become completely qualified. It is a build-up that runs parallel with experience and means that when you are at your peak you are able to move into the top flight and work with the top men, using ideas that the game needs.

That is common sense to me. Too many of our so-called top coaches find themselves in the First Division too quickly. They arrive on the back of a badge and are not ready. They don't have any fresh ideas when, by God, we need them.

I think it is a grave mistake to give the shape of the side, and how they play, to one man. It should certainly not be the coach. What is wrong with the Stock and Gore partnership, or my relationships with Jimmy Andrews and Bill Dodgin? They were not complicated, we didn't try and confuse anyone and the players enjoyed themselves.

I'm old-fashioned and go along with the set-up at Liverpool. Bob Paisley has still got people around him called trainers and they are proving every season that it works. You don't hear much from them either do you? Bob does the talking and they all just get on with it. In Italy they called the trainer's job 'the preparation of man' and that, for me, is about right.

After discussions every day with my right-hand man I

have usually had a refresher course with the players on Friday mornings. We would have worked on different aspects of our play during the week and Friday was their chance to prove that they wanted to use them, and that they could.

It is no good introducing a new plan if the players are not good enough to carry it through. So I took them back to school on Friday, we had an exam. I would stroll out among them and bellow: 'Prove to me that these free kicks you are going to take three yards outside the area are going to work, prove to me that these new corners are effective!' It had to be drummed in.

If it worked we used it, if it didn't we either went through it again or scrapped it. We never used something unless the players were completely happy.

There is just no chance for the manager who doesn't involve himself directly in the way his players are going to operate on match days. Can it be right that you don't know why you have won? And if you don't know why you have lost, that's failure.

Method is one of the over-used words in the coaching vocabulary and yet, quite frankly, it has always meant the same to me. Surely method means getting the maximum effect with the least effort.

All the coaching in the world doesn't hide the fact that the most important job in football is still picking the right team. And that is still the manager's responsibility. He must take the criticism, and possibly the sack, if things go wrong. This is an area where the coach can cheat a little. He can tell people, when things are going wrong and the pressure is on, 'But I don't pick the team, do I? That is nothing to do with me.'

Coaching, quite honestly, is not a difficult job for an intelligent person. Good players adapt very quickly and I just wish some of our respected men with control over players would concentrate more on improving them. Improving skill. That would subsequently improve the team and spread right the way through the game.

There is too much emphasis on tactics and complicated systems. Players don't want to have to worry. All they want to do is enjoy themselves and do the things they are good at.

My role at Bournemouth now takes me to a lot of youth and junior matches and everywhere I go there are coaches. Schoolmasters telling young boys not to do this and not to do that and generally scaring the life out of the poor little devils. Junior clubs playing with sweepers, one and half men up front, no wingers, four across the middle. They are frightened to death of losing, even at their tender age, and it makes me cry. If our game has got any future it is with these boys. Why take the fun out of the game even at such an early age? Where has all the skill gone, strangled by coaches everywhere?

These schoolmasters, youth club leaders and other people with too much control talk in a language that *I* don't even understand. So what hope has the youngster got? And I'm sure they don't really know what they are talking about. Are they using the 'language' to cover up their genuine lack of knowledge?

The one quality our coaches must have is enthusiasm. If you interview a drab man for a coaching job don't employ him. All my men have had an infectious love of the game. When it's raining they must come breezing in and say what a wonderful day it is and when the team have lost badly on Saturday they must be first in on Monday morning, lifting the players, making them forget.

A coach has got to have a big shoulder to cry on and be a lovely bouncy, bright man with not a care in the world. The players have got to look to him for the mood of the day. If he is in a black frame of mind the players will go down with him. He has got to be firm, of course, but on top of his job at all times.

I am very strongly against coaches getting into furious rows with players and having slanging matches out on the training pitch. I have always told my assistants, 'I don't want you belting into players. That is my job. I am the manager and any shouting will be done behind my door.'

Then, when the player has suffered his punishment and comes out with his tail between his legs the coach can lift him. It is then that the club needs the coach most and his powers of man management.

The classic example of 'working together' comes when a manager and his coach are desperately trying to make a success of a group of players that, deep down, they know to be less than the best. They have no money to improve and must squeeze everything possible out of their squad. When it comes right in that situation it is most satisfying, a lovely feeling of achievement.

You search for a pattern that suits the players best, put all your square pegs in the square holes, make sure the balance and the shape of the side is right and lift them to new heights with great powers of persuasion. It's a real team effort, right the way through the club, and that is the system that I have worked all through my career.

What you are trying to do, quite frankly, is to get the players to fit a dream. You know what you want and how you would like to play. It is not always possible, especially when you haven't got the cash, but that is what you are searching for. And the search can go on right the way through your career.

Many times I have signed a player and found that he is not the one after all, he hasn't fitted into the team pattern. It is, of course, not always the best player who makes the team, it is not always the top man who completes the jigsaw. Sometimes you have a fella on your staff who you don't think is very good and who you would be quite happy to let go.

Suddenly, in training, you see him make a tackle or fill in somewhere else in the side and realize that the person you have been searching for has been sitting under your nose. That is a lovely bonus and you might even kid a few people along that you have been working on him for weeks. 'Known about him for a long time' I might say. 'Been keeping him back for the right moment, haven't I?' Just a little bit of kidology didn't hurt anyone and it makes the player feel a bit better.

The assistants I have named, Gore, Dodgin and Andrews,

form another aspect of my career that has made me very proud. They are just some of the players I have signed and have had working under me who have developed their careers and gone on to work at the top.

I saw something in people like Phil Woosham, Bill Taylor, Dave Bowen, Dave Sexton, Alan Mullery, Bill Dodgin, George Petchey, Fred Callaghan, Jimmy Andrews, Mike Keen, Rodney Marsh and Malcolm Macdonald, and many more, and I am delighted that they perhaps learned a little bit from me and went on to use that knowledge in their own careers in football.

I have never called anyone at my clubs 'coaches' and would have bitten anyone's head off who dared call me anything but a manager. At Bournemouth I signed David Webb as team manager and he has a good chance of making it to the top and joining my list of protégés.

At least David is going about it the right way and learning his trade from the bottom. There is no substitute for experience and you don't really need badges and bits of paper. You can pick up technical knowledge from books. It is knowledge of work with players that you need.

So many of today's coaches have arrived in the First Division before their time. There are too many of them with no knowledge, working with the players, who have their fingers on the future of the game. And they are getting extremely well paid for doing a poor job.

I almost gave the Bournemouth job to Rodney Marsh. He was interviewed and we thought long and hard about bringing Rodney back from America and letting him put into practice all his ambitious plans for our game. I have no doubt that Rodney has something to offer (at least he has a strong feeling and love for the English game) although in the end we felt that Webb was better suited to our needs. He is doing well and will go far.

I don't know whether we could survive now without coaches. I just wish they would concentrate on improvement of skills and developing players. There is no need to strangle them all with tactics.

One mystery is that with so many changes and upheavals in the game over the last few years, most of them bad, the coach has lived through it all. Perhaps it is about time the authorities took a long hard look at them and asked themselves exactly what are they contributing to the game. Are they really necessary? And if they stay, my message is, 'Please change'. There is so much flair and fun in football. Don't kill it all off before it's too late.

We need a shake-up, a Messiah with some fresh ideas. Players need a new identity and that can only come from the coaches.

15 Where have all the Players Gone?

If you are totally honest with yourself how many players today excite you, how many of our so-called stars would you make an effort to go and watch? You will have to think long and hard.

Glenn Hoddle and Osvaldo Ardiles definitely, the two Dutchmen at Ipswich, Frans Thijssen and Arnold Muhren, and Kevin Keegan. Now I'm struggling.

Sometimes I look at the England team and wonder how Wembley is consistently sold out. It seems so long ago when the crowd responded to Bobby Charlton's every touch, sat back and admired the cool authority of Bobby Moore, applauded Martin Peters' subtlety and really got behind the whole team. Today there are too many slow handclaps and cries of frustration.

Sadly we are producing too many ordinary players. We are churning out so many players who look and play the game the same way. An old friend of mine Harry Storer had a saying when he looked at a player he didn't fancy. 'No tricks!' And that applies today. Rodney Marsh called them 'grey' players and, on reflection, he was about right. There is not enough colour and excitement about our great game any more.

There are certain managers and coaches who care and others, frightened men – frightened of losing and being sacked – who put winning above everything else, even entertainment. The result is that the game suffers.

Spurs manager Keith Burkinshaw came out with one of the quotes of 1981 as far as I was concerned when he said before the FA Cup Final against Manchester City: 'I hope we win 5-4. Everyone connected with football needs a game like that and a few goals. People are fed up with being bored out of their brains at Wembley. Who wants to see a 0-0 draw on a big occasion?' That was beautiful, my feelings entirely.

The lovely thing was that Keith almost got his wish and Tottenham's exciting 3-2 victory in the replay was one of the matches of the winter, a superb highlight to finish the domestic season on. Fans will remember Ricky Villa's dribble for the winning goal for years and let's hope the excitement and how the public responded will rub off on some of our dull coaches and managers.

Some coaches, of course, want to change the image of the game and haven't got the right players to work with. Our production line is just a conveyor belt of running robots.

There are encouraging signs that we want to change and it needs someone at the top to take the game by the scruff of the neck with a new fresh idea. He has got to throw out a challenge to everyone else. 'There you are, that's what the crowd want. Let's all play like that.' The players too have got to want to change and improve, they have got to start wanting to learn new ideas. I look long and hard at our group of million pound players and, quite frankly, I don't see value for money. Does my little saying – 'Rich men don't sweat' – apply here?

Are our top players too contented? Have they become financially independent of their clubs and managers too early in their careers? What else has the game got to offer them? Money is the big incentive and motivator today and these players have already collected the biggest payday of their lives. Their signing-on fee from a million pound transfer has made them worry-free.

You don't hear much of Ian Wallace, the player Nottingham Forest signed from Coventry. Shouldn't he be scoring goals more regularly, for a striker who cost so much? I wonder if

Brian Clough is entirely happy with that deal and the contribution of the player.

Steve Daley has now gone to America after a period at Manchester City that can only be described as a 'failure'. Can he be content with how he played at Maine Road? Do all our million pound men have a clear conscience?

Andy Gray is another I am worried about, his form concerns me. I still don't see the Gray of old, frightening defences to death and scoring magnificent goals. Surely that is what Wolves manager John Barnwell thought he was signing.

These are only my views, of course, and the managers of the players may be entirely happy. I am sure, however, that the man in the street shares my doubts.

Kevin Reeves, they said, improved in 1980 when his old Norwich manager John Bond took over from Malcolm Allison at Manchester City. 'He is looking good' they told me. Well, I look, and I see no more from Reeves than a player who costs £250,000.

A million pounds, it is an awful lot of money. I think I would expect something special, a player to lift crowds, excite people and bring a few thousand more into the grounds. Quite frankly I would want more for my cash than most of these players have so far produced.

When Ron Atkinson took over at Manchester United he led us into another transfer era by signing Bryan Robson from West Bromwich Albion for £1.7 million. It is a staggering amount of money for one player: I never thought we would see the £2 million star, but we will.

No, I'm afraid we definitely don't bring players up or produce them like we used to. The top players are not as good as we like to dress them up and at the bottom everyone is content with winning instead of development.

Football is all about expression, skill, fun and entertainment; too many players arrive in the Football League with set ways. They have had the skill coached out of them, their natural ability has been stifled. I wonder if coaches can get the slightest thrill from what they are turning out.

When I walked out over Queen's Park Rangers new artificial turf pitch I wondered how many Second Division players would be 'found out' during the 1981-82 season. Sir Stanley Rous, the former FIFA president and a respected stalwart of our game, got it about right when he said: 'All we need now is skill.' That, actually, is a very sad statement because until recently there has always been an abundance of skill in our game.

It is ironic that when I arrived in Italy in 1957 the Roma president said to me 'Inject a little bit of English style into our game. We want to play like you.' I took that as a compliment, and yet a few years later when I was back in England we all seemed to want to play the Continental way. Cautious, afraid of failure. I used to watch teams in Italy and think to myself 'I will never play like that. It's rubbish.'

The greatest player I have ever seen is George Best. I have watched most of our 'greats' in thirty-five years and Best was undoubtedly the tops. He made people get off their backsides and cheer, he was a player for the memory. When George played well you wanted the match to go on and on.

It was a delight just to watch him in training at Fulham. We used to call a halt to a practice match and just sit down and let him get on with what he wanted to do. It was a little bit of education for us all.

Who can dribble today? That may sound an outrageous comment to make but who can you actually name that can take on players and go past them consistently. Peter Barnes of Leeds United is one that comes to mind although, it seems, he is not encouraged enough. One minute he is in the England side and the next he is dropped. Barnes is the kind of player you have got to have complete confidence in and play him.

I have been told many times that now Freedom of Contract is with us there are going to be an awful lot of players available. That is rubbish, there may be a few fellas around but the ones you really want are still like gold dust.

Everyone is searching for the centre forward who can score twenty-five goals a season or the outside left who goes past people and hits magnificent crosses. That kind of player will never be 'up for grabs'.

The difference between today and a few years ago is that the preparation was better. I like to think that we used to be better at making people play. My pet illustration of this is Bobby Keetch. He was rejected as a tearaway by Fulham and everyone said 'You can't possibly be serious' when I signed him. But we made him change, we made him want to improve and in the end he turned out to be a damn good signing. Queen's Park Rangers definitely got value for money.

Keetch obviously liked the good life and I recall one Sunday morning when I unexpectedly popped round to his home just for a chat. Bobby lived in a large block of flats in Putney. I wasn't sure of the number when I got there at about eleven in the morning although there was no need to worry. Three men in suits, who looked like debt collectors, were just getting into the lift and I thought then, 'I'll follow them. I bet I know where they're going.'

Sure enough they led me to Bobby and there he was resplendent in his silk dressing-gown surrounded by black leather furniture and statues of Julius Caesar. 'Not a bad old life Bobby ...' I said when I walked in.

People kept turning up every few minutes, girl friends, mates and other callers. I realized that football and Bobby's private life were two completely separate ways of life. But he knuckled down for me on the pitch and I rate Bobby Keetch as one of my little successes. I gave myself a pat on the back, it was a little victory for man management. 'You have got to want to change, you have got to want to get better.' And he did. Lovely.

Keetch was a character and there are not enough of those around today. The public like to identify with stars, they like a bit of mystery, they want to look in the paper on a Saturday morning and say 'Hey, Jim Smith is playing at Arsenal today, let's go and take a look.'

It used to happen. Not so long ago grown men used to get excited if Manchester United were in town. Charlton, Law,

Best, Crerand, they made you want to stand out in the rain and be part of something special. Kids used to nudge each other if they caught a glimpse of Charlton in the street.

That mystery, sadly, has disappeared today. Television has brought the stars into our homes. Footballers, their goals, their wives, eating habits, shoe-sizes are thrust down our throats until in the end the fan actually believes he knows him. The embarrassed nudge has become a familiar slap on the back 'Hello Bob, how you doing?' The fan doesn't actually have to go to the game to enjoy seeing his hero.

I was told a story recently of how a football fan who had never seen a cup final was offered two free tickets to watch Spurs and Manchester City. 'No thanks', he said. 'I prefer to watch it on television, you see more!'

Footballers, I have discovered over the years, do like discipline. They like routine and to be told what is wrong and right at their club. They like a manager to be strong but fair. They want respect from both sides of the manager's door.

If you have a code of conduct it is important to stick to it at all times. The players expect you to. Even little things like eating habits. A player knows he mustn't return to pre-season training overweight and a few pounds over will mean a fine or other strong action.

Chris Nicholl, whom I signed for Luton from Halifax, was one of the best eaters I have ever met. Most footballers would eat a table if they could and Nicholl was the champion. Cakes, crisps, anything he could get his hands on. But Nicholl was lucky, he didn't put on weight and never had a problem.

Others struggle like mad and you put them on special diets and have them back every day for extra training. 'It's your living' I often screamed at them as they lost weight in the sunshine. 'Keep going.' I have never known a group of people like footballers for eating. A huge evening meal is digested and forgotten by 9.30 p.m. Then they still want endless rounds of sandwiches.

I dream about players, signings, finding a new George Best all day long. When we lived in Epsom I used to begin my day with a stroll across Epsom Downs with my friend and horse trainer Tom Gosling. Every morning he and I used to be out on the Downs at about 6.45, watching the morning appear and talking about our different sports.

He would tell me about horses he had great hopes for and I would mention names of players I would like to sign or couldn't raise the cash for. I enjoyed those walks, it was a good way to start the day. There was no one around at that time, just the new smells of the day, and man's talk. It cleared the air of any pressure you might be feeling and I made a number of decisions about players while out with Tom.

In Bournemouth I now walk around the garden. It's not the same, of course, but old habits die hard. I like to start the day out in the fresh air, just pottering about and thinking life over in general.

I can't help thinking that a club like Bournemouth should be running about ten teams, eight of them full of youngsters who are playing for the fun of it, enjoying life. We should be helping develop their skills; instead they all look so worried about losing.

One of the favourite sayings of a coach is 'He can't play.' My answer is always the same. 'You are talking like a manager, old son, you go and improve him. That is your job, help him through his crisis.'

The chairman of a club should also be involved in this. He is responsible for the image of his team, he should be concerned if he sits up in the stand and watches his side produce football that isn't exciting. If he isn't enjoying himself you can bet that the rest of us are not.

He employs the manager, who employs the coach. It should work all the way down the line. The chairman shouldn't hide, it's his club. He is at the top and has the power to change everything. He shouldn't let a drab standard drift on.

The greatest disloyalty a player can show to his manager, I feel, is criticism behind his back. I have always expressed my disgust at managers who criticize other teams. Well, the same goes for players who rush into print to moan about their own club.

My door has always been open for complaints and rows and I would like to think that every other manager in football is the same. It is an insult to sound off about someone who employs you, especially when they don't know.

Like loud-mouthed managers these players get a reputation and before long they are on a black list. You wouldn't touch them with a barge pole, you are too scared of signing them. Their reputation isn't good. It is far better to wrap your money up in a good character. He may be short of the other bloke's ability but he will give you value for money.

A player should ask himself what his obligations to his club are. Surely it must be to play to the best of his ability and to show respect. When you hear of a £300,000 problem boy, that is criminal.

Oh, for a few more Bobby Moores. No trouble. Just a magnificent player who sets the highest standards. As long as you sat Bob down on the coach after the game and gave him a few lagers he was happy. He wanted the game to come first.

Players, of course, are the backbone of football but they do worry me. It worries me that we are not producing enough good players and concerns me that the individual is not committed enough to the game. He doesn't care enough about his, or football's, image. The rich man. Does he really care when he loses?

Who can give me the answers to my fears? I would like to know why we can't have skill and fun back in football. I would like to know who is trying to destroy our national game.

16 No respect

Ted Drake, the former Chelsea manager and now life president of Fulham Football Club, accompanied me once to a pre-season friendly between Brentford and Millwall. Nothing very significant in that, of course, just a quiet little afternoon out.

We had a couple of drinks in the boardroom after the game, said hello to a few old faces and went home. It was a pleasant evening in early August so we strolled the long way back to the car for a little bit of exercise. The peace of that afternoon was suddenly shattered by a group of supporters, and I use that word very lightly. In fact I'm ashamed to link that particular bunch of kids with football. They were louts and I find it difficult to describe them or their behaviour properly.

They urinated in the street, spat at anyone or anything in sight and charged on to cause more havoc to the innocent. There were about twenty of them, most of them just young boys who on their own wouldn't have dared say a word out of place to anyone. In numbers, however, they were brave little soldiers.

It is a situation that has happened millions of times since and behaviour has become increasingly bad. Two men on their own can't do much about twenty idiots running towards them except think of a solution. On that occasion Ted turned to me and said sadly, 'It makes you want to give up, Alec, doesn't it?' What he meant was how can football managers, schoolmasters, or anyone in authority talk about standards when this kind of thing is happening on the streets, and affecting the public?

And yet Ted did hit the nail firmly on the head. We just mustn't give up fighting back at hooliganism and the new word that has crept up in front of us since the terrible street riots in England during the summer of 1981, yobism. If good people give up and turn their backs on this part of society that is sick, then there is no future for any of us. We have just got to find a solution.

A few years ago it became too easy to call the trouble-maker a 'football hooligan'. He was there in our lives and yet everyone dismissed him as football's problem. It was left to football to solve and the problem was too easily swept under the mat. A number of people in the game tried to give a warning that it had far wider effects. It was a lot more than just fighting at football matches.

Football has, I think and hope, just about got on top of trouble inside its grounds. Outside it is different, and how can a club be responsible for 20,000 supporters travelling home? If they decide to riot an hour after the game and three miles away there is not much a club can do about that.

That is not dismissing the problem or pushing it on to someone else, because, believe me, I am just as worried about this as the next man. If I could have been the one to say 'This is how we beat them' I would have said it long ago. Like everyone in football I talk for hours about rescuing the game from these louts.

It would be interesting to discover exactly where the football hooligan came from. Who invented him, who gave him the title hooligan? There has always been the odd punch-up at football matches. Ever since I can remember, someone in blue has abused someone in red. The difference then was that it all ended quickly with a clip round the ear.

There always was a little bit of respect for authority. If a youngster saw a policeman he would either run away or treat him with esteem. Today I'm afraid a policeman's lot is not a happy one. He is abused, cast as the villain in a number of people's eyes. A young PC is just as likely to finish up with a brick in his eye today; it is a shocking state of affairs.

I suppose it was in the mid-sixties that we saw the birth of the hooligan, the so-called supporter who emerges triumphantly at the end of the game with his scalp of a rival fan's scarf. He has failed unless there has been bloodshed or the outsize toe of his boot has felled some poor bystander.

Was it perhaps the delightful Kop choir at Liverpool that innocently began all this? Their singing and encouraging support became famous country-wide, players began talking about it in public, and television and radio gave the Red Army choir more publicity than perhaps was good for the game.

Did other supporters, jealous of Liverpool's success on and off the pitch, try and emulate the Kop? And when they found they could get nowhere near the same standard of singing or 'entertainment' did they turn to abuse, filthy slogans and foul-mouthed chanting? The obvious development from abuse and bad language is fighting. It is only a thought but somewhere along the line it became fashionable to kick hell out of one another.

You could all probably offer as many solutions to this cancer as I could. Where do we turn, how on earth do we make these animals see sense? They seem to be completely frustrated with life, and violence is their escape.

The Conservative Government supported the police in meeting the street riots with rubber bullets, machines that sprayed dye and jets of water, and stiffer penalties. Good luck to them. Right the way through life there have been people in authority who must make the big decisions and the rest of us, quite frankly, have got to support them. It is no good the Government saying this is what we must do if the opposition immediately tries to prove them wrong before a rubber bullet has been fired.

Authority has got to be in control, hasn't it? The policeman has always been our saviour, our little bit of security. If it was dark and you saw a bobby on the corner you felt a bit better. He may have been frightened out of his wits too but at least his presence was a comfort. And the time has come for us to get behind them again. Give them a little support for a change. The policeman today is literally battling for our future. On the street and on the football terrace he dare not let the hooligan win.

We can all help by standing together and refusing to let these hooligans do as they like. It seems that yobs today exist to break rules. They think they can do exactly as they please. Isn't it time we said 'we dare you to ruin something good'? Isn't it time for us all to stand firm and refuse to be bullied, to get in behind the authorities and support everything they do?

At football matches isn't it time we pointed a few fingers and said 'There he is, there is the one who is causing the trouble'? Isn't it time we stopped thinking that hooliganism is just a phase and something that will disappear soon?

So how do we deal with him, and I am referring now to the football yob in particular. All-seater stadiums they say will bring sanity back to football, although I am not convinced. The hooligan comes in every shape and size now, you know. Money is not his problem, he can afford the best seat in the place if he wants it. If the hooligan and his mates want to go to a football match for a punch-up there is no guarantee that an all-seater stadium will deter him.

I have only ever been forced to ban two people from any of my football clubs, one was a schoolmaster, the other a company director. That is not trying to make light of the problem we are talking about, it only proves that if people want to make trouble they will.

Stiffer punishment. Definitely. I was brought up to accept that discipline meant loss of privilege. I was frightened to step out of line, and if I did I knew that I would suffer. How do you make a hooligan suffer? It's not easy I admit. Have we got to frighten them a bit to make them realize that there is a bit of authority still in existence. Police with dogs, I have always thought, broke up the party quite quickly. And the local courts have got to be given complete backing to hand out the kind of punishment that will make the yobs think twice about repeating their revolting behaviour. Some of the fines at the moment are laughable, so small that they pay it out of their pockets on the spot. It once cost one of my clubs £200 to summons a trouble maker and he was eventually fined £15.

Whatever crackdown we do employ it is late in coming. It has got to a stage where, if we are not careful, the hooligan defeats *you.* He can choose his time; his actions seem to be well organized, and it's frightening. They are saying to themselves when, where and who.

Until recently it was left to football to sort out this problem. People stood back and said it is your responsibility, you must control what is happening. Suddenly all of us in football are looking for guidance again. We have been proved right, hooliganism is an evil part of society that affects us all. We said all along that it was impossible just to link it with sport and the summer riots of 1981 sadly proved us right.

Now football authorities fear that the new kind of terror, the organized crime, will spill over to them. How on earth do you cope with that inside a ground?

It has got to be a question of much tougher methods, tougher punishment and backing for authority. The yobs have got to be scared. They probably don't know the meaning of respect but, old-fashioned as that might be, that is what we are talking about.

Inside football clubs the good guys have got to come to a decision. If we want someone to destroy it, then stand back. No, on the streets and inside our grounds, we have got to stand firm and say 'We enjoy this sport, we enjoy watching football here, we enjoy living here, and you are not going to take that from us.' It will probably need an almighty confrontation but why should we allow them to win. Whatever action the authorities take, and I hope it's damn tough, I am right behind them. There is no other way.

Discipline in football clubs too could be a little tougher. Players today are in danger of becoming molly-coddled. Whatever wrong they do, it doesn't really seem to affect them. Do they really care? When a player was suspended he never used to get paid. He lost privilege, it was his punishment. Today they get away scotfree, the Players Union have seen to that and I wonder if it is right.

Can it be good that a player doesn't have to worry about losing money? Surely there should be a corner in everyone's life when they say to themselves, 'I mustn't do that because I will be punished'? Are we all going soft? Very indirectly, has the footballer lost a little respect for his profession?

The two talking points of this chapter are not linked, of course, but they are problems I have been worried about for a long time. The player is perhaps too well protected by his union, he has become untouchable.

With hooliganism, what we are talking about is the changing and breaking of rules.. The hooligan is no longer scared to walk down a London street and throw a brick through someone's window. We have almost accepted it as part of a new era.

It has certainly brought this terrible problem to a head and it's time to fight back. If we don't I fear for the future in this country. The next time two men face twenty yobs in a Brentford Street they might not live to tell the story!

17 Too Many Critics

Jimmy Hill, football voice of the BBC, and Brian Moore, Independent Television's top soccer commentator, are sitting in unique positions. And never before in the history of football have two men had so much power and such difficult roles to play.

Jimmy, of course, swaps analysis, criticism and comment in the board meetings at Coventry where he is managing director while Brian is a director of Third Division Gillingham. They are both steeped in the history of football and possess knowledge of and a great feeling for the game. Their integrity is not to be challenged. But the problem they have to reconcile is how to serve two masters.

In an era when we are desperately seeking to repair the image of football in this country do Hill and Moore sometimes find it difficult to fall on one side of the fence? If the BBC feels that some rough criticism is needed for football, is Hill's conscience clear if he dishes it out?

What would happen if there was crowd trouble or something went drastically wrong with security during a match at Coventry and Hill knew his club were responsible? Jimmy would have to make a big decision; would he criticize his own club in the same way as he has hit hard at others, or would he decide to soft pedal?

For me it is a very interesting talking-point. I care very much about football in this country, I worry about the image and style of the game and the people who run it and play it.

My responsibilities are completely for football, nothing else. I wonder where Jimmy and Brian, two very experienced and highly efficient fellas, put theirs. Do they feel that television, which provides their living, is their ruler?

Or is it football? When they are talking about the game in front of millions of people do they sometimes think to themselves 'Is it safe to say that? Am I open to criticism?' When Brian Moore is criticizing England up front in the commentary box, is he talking as a director as well as a member of the media?

As a director, after all, he is a man who, indirectly, is responsible for the running and therefore the image of the game. Can he help to sack a manager in the boardroom on Tuesday night and then swap hats on Saturday and talk about the behaviour of others in football, without feeling guilty?

This isn't criticism of the two fellas. It is just the best possible way in which I can illustrate a part of football that often concerns me, the coverage the game receives through television and newspapers. The media has a huge influence on the people and politics of football. Jimmy and Brian have a problem but I just hope that at the end of the day they strike the right balance between their jobs and their clubs.

I have already said that I believe there is too much televised football on our screens and I support that by fearing that the influence of the box is too great. Is it a question of people on the fringe of the game becoming too powerful?

I am not talking about Hill and Moore now, but the men who package the hours of televised football we see every season. I doubt very much if they care at all about what is happening to the national game. While everyone is talking about dwindling gates they just want to get more live coverage on the screens.

It always used to be just the game we saw while standing on the terrace. Now there are hundreds of television spin-offs, playbacks, golden goal competitions, save of the season, quiz games, panels, interviews, documentaries; the sport is pulled inside out and if we are not very careful there will be no guts to play with. There is no mystique left, as I have said. The cameras are allowed everywhere.

We have now even got the interview with First Division managers in the dug-out on the touchline or from their grandstand seat at the start of the second half. 'What do you think of it so far?' they are asked. Rubbish, that is what I think of this new development. Isn't there anything sacred left? How much further can we take this new exposure?

During the 1980-81 season Manchester City allowed the TV cameras into their ground for a documentary called *City*. It featured the going of Malcolm Allison and coming of John Bond. Of course there is nothing to hide but why should the public be allowed in. The fans' interest was surely always held by not quite knowing what went on behind the locked doors of a football club. In the end, I suppose, it comes down to money. If the price is right people will do anything these days.

That programme was a marvellous scoop for television, although I wonder if City chairman Peter Swales and his directors were delighted with the outcome. Did they really want the world to see their interview of Bond or the boardroom discussion that followed? Allison, according to the programme, left on a wave of player sympathy and almost regret. You were left asking the question: Why did he go? I just can't see how that programme did the game any good.

The big weekend football programmes on Saturday night and Sunday afternoons have also introduced tittle-tattle news items, the kind of stories that were always reserved for the Sunday newspapers. Those stories in print, instantly followed up by the morning reporters, always produced the tongue-in-cheek reaction 'Never believe what you read in the papers.' It was a convenient get-out on a Sunday afternoon if you had your feet up and the phone rang. Are we now to use the same excuse for television. 'Never believe what you see on the box.'

Television producers are well aware that far more people

are swayed and convinced by pictures than words. They make up their minds instantly about something and someone, identify with people they have never met. So I just hope that when television runs its next gossip story it had better be right.

The power of the media was brought stunningly home to me when I read comments from the Manchester United chairman Michael Edwards when his club were searching for a replacement for sacked Dave Sexton. 'Among the new man's qualities' United said 'is that he must be able to cope with the media.' I begin to wonder what's happening.

Television once did me a marvellous favour, however, in the transfer market. Fulham were involved in Saturday's *Match of the Day* programme and one of my strikers, who had been having a bit of a rough time, came over superbly on the box. He looked a million dollars and as I sat in my armchair I wondered if anyone else would have been impressed.

You would be surprised how many managers and chairmen look at televised football and make up their minds about a player. For some it is their weekend scouting. And sure enough, after a Sunday telephone call, I sold my centre forward the following day. I'm not saying he wasn't worth the price I got but that televised clip of his goals and performance certainly helped.

Players do worry if they know the cameras are 'outside'. The buzz goes round the dressing-room and you can sense them saying to themselves, 'It is essential I play well today'.

Supporters too are easily influenced by television. A poor pass by Bobby Moore, his only one of the game, would bring out the Sunday comment over a pint: 'Old Moore didn't look so good last night.' Yet one cracking centre that led to goal from a player who hadn't done a thing in the entire game, can turn him into a hero. 'What a ball, didn't so and so play well.' You can't stop that kind of thing happening but it does concern me a little. Television can cloud the truth.

We are talking about instant personalities and that is what

television produces. Players and managers are dropped into our living room and then forgotten as our next hero comes along. It is a very powerful business.

Newspapers, television and communicating with the media are part and parcel of a manager's life. Some managers enjoy it, others do it because they have to, while others like Sexton, clearly don't put handling of the media high up on their list of qualities or priorities.

I can't excuse anyone who doesn't talk to the press, because they have a very major role to play in the game. I just can't see how it should be taken into consideration when you are hiring and firing.

I have always had a little personal rule as far as the press are concerned and that is 'Have something happening'. Managers have a responsibility to the public and newspapers are a route to open up a relationship. So I have always found it important to be available and make sure there has been a talking-point.

Usually a reporter knows what he wants before he picks up the telephone so there is absolutely no point in saying 'No comment'. And if there is nothing happening, make it. And if it's bad, don't tell him to write it good. Always be fair and, hopefully, if there is a little grey area one day when he is reporting or doing a story then he might just come down on your side.

My one criticism of popular newspapers and their reporters is that there is too much criticism. Managers, players, chairmen and directors do pay a lot of attention to what is written about them, they can be hurt by criticism and feel a million dollars just because an article has praised a performance or a goal. It is hard to understand, I know, but it is true.

In the *Sunday People* newspaper every weekend they give a number out of ten for every player from every match they cover. You will be surprised how many stars turn to that page before they read anything else over breakfast. If the mark is high they will be lifted for the day. It is extraordinary. If a manager says 'I never read newspapers' it is almost certain that he is not telling the truth. Every manager in football reads newspapers.

I have no sympathy either with the manager who, faced with a group of pressmen after one of his players has been sent off or involved in a controversial incident, says that he didn't quite see the incident. Of course, he saw it. He is just hiding.

But I do have sympathy with the man who is criticized unjustly by newspapers, by reporters who perhaps don't have enough knowledge. Alf Ramsey and recently Ron Greenwood are two outstanding cases that spring to mind, of managers who have come under the power of the press hammer.

What most people in the game want from the media is authority. I am not talking about transfer stories and the everyday news that makes up a reporter's world but authority to tell us something new. Constructive authority rather than blind criticism.

Most other sports have someone with a complete knowledge of the game. Why not football? Where is the man to send me rushing down stairs in the morning just to read his report of a game, or his comments on a certain talking-point? We all still want to be educated.

There is an assumption, I am sure, that most people want to read twaddle about football. Who said what, how unhappy Jim Smith is, what a player did on Saturday night. That could not be further from the truth; most people want constructive journalism. The supporter too wants more these days than just tit-bits. He wants to say 'Yes, I agree' or 'What a lot of rubbish so and so is talking about today'.

There is far more criticism about the game now than there has ever been before. Why? There are so many good points to expose although I do appreciate that criticism will probably sell more newspapers than praise. Perhaps this chapter is directed at the sports editors and the men who control what goes in the pages and hand out the directives. So I ask them: 'Are we not moving away from the smash bang horror story era and moving towards more balanced reporting?'

Other sports don't tear their fellas to bits although it seems to be an unwritten law in football. But if that is what the sports editor wants and thinks best for his paper who am I to argue. And it would take a strong, and probably foolish, journalist to say to his sports editor, 'No I am not writing it that way, this is what we should do.'

I suppose my fears all relate to knowledge. If you haven't got a deep love of the game and a wide knowledge to back it up you can't write constructively. You can only criticize.

The Football League, they say, are worried about too much television and the media's general handling of our sport. There is not, quite frankly, a lot you can do about it. Football is a game involving public opinion and television and newspapers are a very important part of the set-up. What we must hope for is that some people change. That people who influence others have new fresh ideas about a sport that needs very careful handling in the next few years.

I like to think my track record with journalists is good. My door has always been open and I have always been available right round the clock. I can never understand managers who won't talk to the press or keep them standing around in car parks or corridors or instruct commissionaires to block off access to players.

Everyone has a role to play and the time has come surely to pull together. Let's stop knocking football. It is a marvellous sport that gives an awful lot of people a very good living.

Football, right the way through from the England side to clubs like Bournemouth in the Fourth Division, needs more support and praise than it has been receiving over the last few years.

18 The Future

If we are not careful English football is again in danger of turning our most important manager into a failure. Like Sir Alf Ramsey and Don Revie before him, Ron Greenwood is finding the system difficult to beat as England manager, and with typical English reaction the vultures are after him. What a wonderful thing for Ron that England qualified for the 1982 World Cup at the last minute. It was his turn to say, 'We did it the hard way', and success kept the critics off his back.

It is staggering to me how we treat the England manager. Instead of giving him support and backing we take great delight in using him as the scapegoat when things go wrong. Ramsey is the classic example. The only man to win the biggest prize of all, the World Cup, is now just forgotten. Sacked, humiliated, it's unreal.

The Football Association has a lot to answer for in its handling of the Ramsey situation. I think it got away scotfree with a terrible piece of mismanagement. No other country in the world would have said to a man, 'You won us the World Cup, you have lifted us right up there with the rest, you have worked hard and gained respect throughout the world. Now out. We don't want you or your methods any more.'

The contempt they showed for him was the climax of a witchhunt that this country is very good at. And the only one to come out of the shambles with any credit was Sir Alf. How he didn't show his true feelings or reveal his bitterness I will never know. I'm sure he is still a very frustrated man, especially when he sees and hears the sympathy being offered now to all Greenwood's problems. They were only the same kind of setbacks that Ramsey always lived with.

I still can't believe that the Football Association never used his great knowledge after getting rid of him as manager. As in so many cases before him, and since, the experience and knowhow of a football manager is wasted.

Is it too much to hope that the World Cup began a new era for English football? England's victories against Hungary in 1981 probably saved Greenwood from a massive new campaign for his head which, quite frankly, he probably wouldn't have survived. If we are good at one thing in this country, it is putting people under pressure. Greenwood's knowledge of the world game is second to none and he is a fine manager. But we will toss him aside, just like the rest if, as is expected, he quits the job after the World Cup Finals in Spain in 1982.

If Greenwood's reign has done one thing, however, it is to highlight the problem that our England manager has to live with. People are so fed up with us not winning, qualifying or playing exciting football that everyone is turning the spotlight on to the reasons why.

The repercussions of the England job, and the results we achieve, the standard the team sets and the effect it has on people throughout the country make it, of course, the most important aspect of our game. It is the key to our future and, quite frankly, we must get it right.

Everything starts with England. The standard is set there. If we get the England set-up right then we have got a chance in the future. And to get it right it is obvious to everyone that there have got to be changes, big, drastic changes. The structure and the system have to be beaten. Someone, somewhere, in a position of power in our great game has got to decide that if we want our international football to rise again to the highest plane then we have got to do things to get it there.

We have got to decide whether we are going to support England or vote for club football. At the moment our game is geared around club football and England 'fits in' when we can get the dates and the players together at the same time. England is a hit-and-miss run outfit and we are missing. So if we decide to hit we change and the biggest change of all must be to streamline the First Division to eighteen clubs and regionalize the Third and Fourth Divisions. There is no other way.

We play too much football at the moment. There is never time for anything; time for England, time for preparation of young players, time for proper coaching. We have got into a bit of a mess and we have got to get out of it fast. When the changes come, and they are likely to be after Greenwood's reign as England manager, there seems to be only one man for the England job and that is Brian Clough.

It is going to be such an important period for our football that we will need a strong man, a person who can beat the system, a person who doesn't mind taking knocks and hurting others. He will have to say, 'I'm sorry, you have been around for a long time, but things are changing around here and if *you* won't then you are out, old son. Your cushy little life is over.'

It is tough and ruthless but these men in authority didn't show Ramsey the same kind of feeling. Clough, given complete support, could just about do it. I have no fears about his ability; it is whether he could survive the turmoil and back-stabbing that will undoubtedly come when someone says 'Right, this is what we are going to do. And it affects you, you and you. Out.'

So who are these men with the power to change our course and put us back on the road to success. Significantly two new faces emerged at the start of the 1981-82 season and the responsibility lies with them. We are looking towards them to lead us into a new era.

Jack Dunnett, the Notts County chairman and Member of Parliament for Nottingham East, is the new President of the Football League. Bert Millichip, the solicitor and chairman of West Bromwich Albion, was elected to succeed Sir Harold Thompson as Chairman of the Football Association in June

1981. These men have got to show the way and the early signs are good, thank heavens.

They both started their new roles at the same time, and that is encouraging. They must work hand-in-hand to bring the FA and League closer together and revolutionize the game. Ever since the days of Sir Stanley Rous we have looked for leadership and now these two new faces have got a chance to go down in history as the men who saved our national game.

What we want most is to see them and hear them taking notice of everyone, big and small, in football. I have worked nearer than most managers to the Football Association at Queen's Park Rangers and Fulham and yet never really saw anyone from Lancaster Gate.

In my quiet moments I thought 'They must all be busy up there' but never really understood what they were doing. Now they have got to show they care. We are expecting great things this time, not just chat.

Lord Westwood and Sir Harold Thompson were Jack Dunnett and Bert Millichip's predecessors and, with all due respect, when did they actually make you sit up and listen? When did we actually say: 'What a damn good idea'?

Our two new leaders have now got to show us that they care about the future of the game. They, and the people below them, have got to show that the game is more important to them than their roles in it. We don't want closed doors and secret committee meetings going on all the time. We want decisions and action. And if they have got to move stubborn people then that is the way it has got to be. For the good of the game a lot of people have got to be asked, 'What have you done all these years?' Jack and Bert must challenge them. The dead wood must go.

They must realize that our football is getting worse in relation to other countries. The rest are either getting better and we are standing still or, as I fear, we are going backwards. Now we must stand in the way of the tide and force it back again.

Attention first should be focused on the England set-up

and a cut-back to the First and Second Divisions. That is the biggest job of all and, quite frankly, if they succeed in changing that system it will be one hell of an achievement.

Streamlining sounds simple but just look at the complications. The accepted number in a reduced First Division seems to be eighteen. That means four clubs have got to be told 'Sorry, but you are no longer in the top flight. You must be relegated.' It means they must swallow the fact that they can no longer look forward to entertaining the top teams and top players. Their crowds will go down and with it their income.

Then to make the streamlining work there obviously must be one season with no promotion. It is no good dropping four clubs out of the First Division if another three come back in. So the three top clubs at the top of the Second Division must also be told 'Sorry, you have done well but you can't go up.'

After that little bit of surgery we are left with twenty-six clubs in the Second Division. Too many. So, if we want eighteen in the Second Division as well, eight of those clubs have got to be relegated. I certainly wouldn't like to be the bloke who tells them, but if it is streamlining we want, and I see no alternative, then that is what must happen.

The directive for that kind of decision must come from Jack Dunnett and his Management Committee. And if they solve that little lot then they will go down in football history. There are so many mountains to climb and the mountains are the clubs themselves. The attitude is sure to be 'I'm all for change, but why me? I didn't think you meant us.'

The First and Second Division chairmen get the final vote at the League's annual meeting, and will they vote each other out? I doubt it. The old pals act would close ranks so tightly that Dunnett and his men would probably have to scamper away for another massive rethink.

I have thought long and hard about this problem and still can't come up with a better alternative. The new President stood up at the annual meeting after he was elected and said that the England team manager must be able to pick the best players. Hear, Hear. Now let him. That is the problem.

Every England manager has been fed up with club officials putting themselves first, players dropping out at the last minute and only being able to prepare for vital matches for a couple of days. The obvious way to help them is to play fewer matches and give the England manager more access. If we want a successful International team we have got to be fair to the manager.

After streamlining at the top must come regionalization at the bottom. I just can't see any argument against it. For the good of the smaller clubs we must cut back on their travelling expenses and give them more local derbies to attract more people into the grounds. For the minnows at the moment we are running a product with no appeal. The only appeal is to get out!

A few weeks after I joined Bournemouth they said we were playing our local derby at Torquay. It was a 7.30 p.m. kick-off for some reason, and after we had stopped for fish and chips on the way home (Fourth Division clubs just can't afford big four-course slap-up meals) we arrived back at Bournemouth at 1.30 on Sunday morning. I said to the chairman 'Harold, that was lovely, I am pleased to have been on your local derby!'

That is the kind of problem that clubs like Bournemouth are facing. Until football supports us we are dead and before the 1981-82 season the Bournemouth chairman said that the writing was on the wall. 'The next season is going to make or break us.' I know for a fact that the same message was being transmitted in a number of other boardrooms.

How can football say to Bournemouth: 'Good luck next season, your nearest game is Aldershot. You haven't got any matches in London, and have a nice time travelling to Blackpool and Darlington.' I think I have got my figures right when I say that last season seventeen of our twenty-three away matches meant leaving on Friday night. We really play in the old Third Division North!

It has got to the stage where it is a desperate fight to stay in existence. You work damned hard for a year and are happy just because the club's head is above water. We just can't do any more travelling to places like Darlington and Hartlepool. It has simply got too expensive to make it worthwhile.

Bournemouth's problem, of course, is highlighted by the fact that we are slap bang in the middle of a very expensive area. We haven't got a working-class community that responds to a football club, we haven't got a nucleus of support that the club can rely on. I am not just crying for Bournemouth, it is a problem that a lot of clubs are facing. Football, at the bottom, has never been so hard up.

If the clubs in the Third and Fourth Division are not given regionalization I predict that inside two years a number of them will be part-time. If football won't help them, they must help themselves. It is the only way to cut back on costs; the only step left. It will also be a sad day for the game because I don't believe that the Football League will be enhanced by having part-time players; it can't possibly help build bigger and better soccer in this country.

There will also be terrific problems for the clubs before they can see and gain any reward. They must find jobs for the part-time players which guarantee them the same amount of money and then rely on them being available for all matches. In an era of high unemployment who can guarantee that a group of 'unskilled' footballers will be able to pick up jobs just like that?

I sincerely hope that the Football League understands the problems of a Fourth Division club. And if they don't take action to help them soon, it will be too late.

There are other aspects of football that I don't understand, little mysteries that remain unsolved. Obvious things, yet I can't quite discover why they never happened. Like ground sharing.

When I was manager at Queen's Park Rangers I used to look out of my office window at Loftus Road and see the White City Stadium standing there, unused and empty. Two stadiums touching one another and yet so far apart. I wondered who it was that refused to let them be turned into one big beautiful sports project. A stadium that could have been used by the public every day of the week, a real money-spinning concern.

The big clubs now, of course, are too independent to share. It is at the bottom of the pile where it makes sense and Bristol is the prime example. Why Bristol City and Bristol Rovers have not got together I will never know. I suppose we are talking about people again, little empires that might be sent crashing to the ground.

On paper an amalgamation of two small clubs in the same city makes sense but do the individual people concerned want it? Does the chairman of one club suddenly realize that he can no longer hold his position in a sharing scheme, are their committees frightened of change? All through football I fear that there are people who are holding up progress.

On the Continent most of the sports stadiums belong to the public. They are used as mass sports empires for the family and this is what we must start to move towards in this country. It is no good thinking we can turn football clubs into sports complexes because at most grounds there just isn't the scope or space; most stadiums would have to be flattened and built again for that to happen.

Any club, however, which builds a new stand or clubhouse in the future must consider other sports and ways of using it to attract a complete cross-section of the public. Squash courts, bowling alleys, restaurants, anything to bring in people seven days a week.

I would like to see local authorities take more interest too in football clubs in their area. Why shouldn't they help if their public are going to use the facilities? Multi-sports centres cost big money I know but they simply must be a part of our future. The football stadium as we know it is no longer a moneymaking workable proposition.

These are all aspects of the game that Dunnett and Millichip must put into a bag and shake up. The entire structure of football is now under review and the answers must be positive. We have let the problems slowly build up and right now we have reached the crossroads. One more wrong turn could prove disastrous.

I can see a problem too with our transfer market. Suddenly over the past few years managers have had to go abroad for bargains because of the spiralling prices here and players like Ardiles, Villa, Thijssen and Muhren have proved to be superb successes. Now, I ask, how many foreign players can we allow in?

We must never forget that the transfer market is the lifeblood of the small clubs. It is our only way to improve and we mustn't find ourselves in a situation where there are not enough players circulating.

There is also a danger that the public is going to expect a bit of wizardry from an Ardiles and put a manager under pressure to go abroad for a new face, a name to make his fans satisfied.

Cricket has suffered at the hands of this problem and the complaint for years is that we don't have any English fast bowlers coming through to take over, or there are no middle order batsmen with class. I wouldn't like to hear people saying in England that all the top-class players in this country are foreign.

I believe, therefore, that as in cricket we must restrict the number of imports any one club can have on its books. I think one, and certainly no more than two, is enough.

The transfer fees must also be controlled. We must never allow the price of players to go through the roof again, we must never have an explosion like the million-pound shock or the prices paid in the 1980-81 and 1981-82 seasons. There is no logic in it – although I know that some madman somewhere would pay it again if prices took off once more. As I was writing this book Manchester United paid almost two million for West Brom's Bryan Robson. And, as before, the ball will roll right the way through the game. Other managers will say 'If he is worth two million my lot are worth just as much.'

Once again there will be ordinary players changing hands for astronomical amounts. Everyone says 'Let's control the market' when they are really thinking 'I hope I have got someone who is worth a few million.' Then the most dangerous thing of all happens. The player himself believes he is worth that much. I have already said that Freedom of Contract has destroyed management and it is ironic and damned unfair that it has been introduced just when players believe they can get away with the earth.

I have always thought that Freedom of Contract is a little piece of blackmail and I have been proved right straight away. The player is only interested in himself, not his club. He wants the best possible offer and doesn't care if his manager has to wait until just before the start of the season for an answer.

Can it be right that a manager, when he is looking for peace of mind and stability before the start of the season, is left with a huge gap in his first team squad? To me that is a hopeless piece of football administration and if we are talking about the future and progress then we must surely do better than this. A man needs his tools to do a proper job and a manager's tools are his players. It is impossible to pick up replacements at the last minute.

It is a crazy business, isn't it, when the most powerful person in football is suddenly the player? He is holding the game to ransom. The Professional Footballers' Association no doubt are happy and it is the manager again who suffers. We must surely get back to the situation where someone in authority has control.

Management, as we know it, is disappearing. We can take a line from Coventry here and they are setting a new image with Jimmy Hill sitting upstairs with the power and Dave Sexton down on the pitch with the players.

It is split command and a situation I expect to see repeated at a number of other First Division clubs in the near future, although I am against it. The club owner will soon be joined on the board by a paid director; a man not, as we thought, from football. He will be an outside businessman and they will run the club together.

I believe it was Southampton's fine young manager, Lawrie McMenemy, who said that he started out ten per cent a manager and ninety per cent a coach. Now the roles have been reversed and I can see Lawrie being forced to give way. He will become so wrapped up in the image of his club and the game that he will soon have to employ a coach to look after the tactics and playing side completely.

Management is disappearing, and for someone like me who has always enjoyed the wheeling and dealing part of the club, someone who has always wanted to be involved in upstairs and downstairs, it is sad. I have always vowed that to manage is the difficult part of running a football club.

I don't know what Jack Dunnett and Bert Millichip have in mind although I am sure it is for the good of the game. We must have changes, everyone knows that. This time they have got to be right. Men in power have been talking for years and the end product is still struggling along under a survival cloud.

There have been changes but we have still only managed to make the game increasingly drab. Bigger promotion with three up and three down, Freedom of Contract, three points for a win, who can argue that they have helped push football back up the ladder?

The changes now must come from people. Individuals who have been snoozing away in little corners of the game must be brushed out and told to wake up or be ruthlessly kicked out. Dunnett and Millichip have got to do that. They mustn't be kind. The time has come to ask a lot of people in high places: 'What exactly have you been doing all these years? How have you helped football? Do you care?'

The Management Committee and FA Council are two other grey areas I don't completely understand. Why don't we have more former managers filling these seats? Why aren't managers encouraged to make decisions that will influence the game?

I once was at a meeting where Bob Lord, the former Burnley chairman and a very powerful man in football, was the guest speaker. All the top brass were there and halfway through his speech Lord said, 'I am all for secretaries, I am all for players, I am all for referees, but managers? Never.' It staggered me and he never went on to explain. Why? Is that a feeling that runs through football? Are the powers that be frightened of us? Do they realize that we know what the game needs and must have? In every walk of life there is a demand for management. Business is screaming for it. Why doesn't football want it?

Football is a game of public opinion, it is what a supporter thinks about his team, his manager, his players. The game belongs to the public and if they don't like what they see then it is time to change. That time has arrived and the trouble in this country is that we have created a monster. We have produced a game that the public doesn't understand, so the simple reaction is to stay away. Who can blame them? You pay your money, and take your choice. Our supporter wants to see a bit of excitement and style about his team again.

Perhaps it would be better if we threw away the coaching manual for a couple of seasons and allowed players to play with a bit of freedom. Why not have two wingers? The fans and the players are browned off with the laws that throw us all into the same hat. We want characters and expression, goals and thrills. There is no substitute.

Messrs Dunnet and Millichip face a monumental task, of course, and they will never be able to do it without the goodwill of others. There have got to be sacrifices and that is when they will run into trouble. But we are looking for the miracle man and, quite frankly, it has got to be one of our two new leaders.

It is up to us all, everyone connected with football, to help them produce a game that once more catches the imagination of the public. We have all got to work together and if the message comes through that you have got to step down, move over or get out then, old son, that is what you have got to do. For the good of football there can be no such word as 'No' again.

Dunnett has already gone on record as saying that it will take his three years of office to start to get things moving in the right direction. He will need all of that. In one of our emotional moments Harry Zussman once said to me 'They should give you the VC for what you have done for my club.'

Well, Dunnett will deserve a knighthood if he sorts out all our problems.

If between them they don't succeed then football must look elsewhere for a leader, one man who can take the game by the cruff of the neck, knock the League and the Football Association into a cocked hat and come up with the answers. I don't believe that man is in football at the moment. If he was we would have produced him and put him on a pedestal already. No, he would have to come from outside the game, a man with a business brain who doesn't mind upsetting people. A man who is good at managing!

Dunnett and Millichip must first be given a chance and complete support. We don't want words anymore, we need and must have action. We mustn't have faceless men standing in the way of progress. We must have authority and decisions. Never before have two new faces emerged up front at such an important time. I hope they succeed because football has been my life and I will always care about the greatest game in the world.

I fear that my kind of role in football, the out and out manager, is going to disappear but if that is for the good of football and progress then so be it.

People are my main worry, the kind of people who I haven't understood throughout my career – stubborn, dangerous types who think only of themselves. I have refus to be trodden on by them and I hope that our two new leaders feel the same way.

I have always maintained that football is all about a little thing called pride and if Dunnett and Millichip have pride in what they are doing we should be all right. I so desperately want a new era to open up for all the good guys around.

And now that I have retired from management I would like to be able to sit back and say that I helped build a little bit of football in this country. I want to say that I contributed to management, to the game. I would like, always, to be able to say: 'Football is not a bad old life really, is it? Hmmm. Go out and enjoy yourself, old son.'

Appendix: Career Dates

Alec Stock's career in management began in 1946 when he joined Southern League Yeovil Town as player manager. Below, in brief, is his journey through the toughest job in football.

May 1949	Yeovil to Orient
Feb 1956	Orient to Arsenal
April 1956	Arsenal to Orient
July 1957	Orient to Roma
Nov 1957	leaves Roma
March 1958	returns to Orient
March 1959	quits Orient
June 1959	joins Queen's Park Rangers
Nov 1968	sacked by Queen's Park Rangers
Dec 1968	joins Luton
June 1972	joins Fulham
Dec 1976	quits Fulham
April 1977	back at Queen's Park Rangers as a director
July 1978	Queen's Park Rangers caretaker manager
Jan 1979	joins Bournemouth as manager
Oct 1981	retires as manager of Bournemouth but continues as a director